M000028341

You Are Not Alone

Our Loved Ones Are Here ... You're Just Not Listening

By Sydney Sherman

BART
BRYANT
PRODUCTIONS

Some names and identifying details have been changed to protect the privacy of individuals.

Although the author and publisher have made every effort to ensure that the information in this book was correct at press time, the author and publisher do not assume and hereby disclaim any liability to any party for any loss, damage, or disruption caused by errors or omissions, whether such errors or omissions result from negligence, accident, or any other cause.

You Are Not Alone

Our Loved Ones Are Here... You're Just Not Listening

© Copyright 2012 by Sydney Sherman
All rights reserved, including the right to reproduce this book, or portions thereof, in any form.

Cover Photography Copyright © 2011 by Billy Boyce Photography
Cover Design, Book Design and Editing by E. J. Northrop

Bart Bryant Productions Durham Road Madison, CT 06443

BART
BRYANT
PRODUCTIONS

ISBN: 978-0-615-64202-4

Library of Congress Control Number: 2012939970

First Edition, June 2012

Printed in USA

Contents

Preface

Dedication

Acknowledgements

Chapter 1 ... Who Am I?

Chapter 2 ... How Important Could It Be?

Chapter 3 ... Through My Eyes... What Do I Experience?

Chapter 4 ... Myths About Life After Death... Sorting Out the Significance

Chapter 5 ... What Makes Us Believe?

Chapter 6 ... A Society of Believers... An Informal Survey

Chapter 7 ... I Want to Believe... Why We Believe

Chapter 8 ... How Do They Touch Our Lives? (Case Histories) ... Are They What's Missing?

Chapter 9 ... How Can I Talk to My Loved Ones?

Chapter 10 ... The Reader... What You Need to Know About Readers

Chapter 11 ... More About the Reader... The Energy of Things

Chapter 12 ... Touched by an Angel... How Do They Help Us?

My Family Gallery

Reader Checklist

Testimonials

Preface

The writing of this book has been a long time in coming.

It has long been my desire to share my personal experiences in order to demystify the paranormal occurrences in our lives. I decided to embark on this journey to provide clarity and understanding while debunking the false impressions left by the media.

In recent years a number of successful popular films and pieces of literature have focused the public's curiosity on the paranormal. It is this increased general interest in paranormal activity, ghosts, ghost hunting and the afterlife that provoked me to follow this path *now,* but the longstanding motivation for this journey has always been to promote greater understanding.

For one whom felt the need to keep a part of my life secret for many years, this increased awareness in things beyond our normal experience is truly amazing. It's a very exciting time for me and many others in the paranormal field.

Having a greater number of people open to the paranormal is very gratifying. That people are willing to accept the possibility of another part of life or a connection to the "other side" is, for me, a validation.

The descriptions of events, activities and especially the motivations in the whole realm of spirit-human interaction have been so misrepresented by entertainment industries. I feel the need to replace imagination and speculation with information.

It seems as if rationality or any scrap of common sense is overshadowed by what I like to call the "media scare effect". It's not done maliciously, but can cause harm nonetheless.

The entertainment industry has created a perfect place for you to go for your paranormal needs. Unfortunately, the information, or rather, misinformation, provided is for entertainment purposes only. Now, in itself, that is not destructive. I too enjoy these types of shows, movies, etc. As a matter of fact, I am grateful to some of the shows for bringing the topic of the afterlife to the forefront.

The damage in entertainment's portrayal of the paranormal is what is omitted. They leave out some very important facts and the valuable possibilities the paranormal holds for us. Yes, spirits do exist. And contact can be made with them. However, most spirits, especially the energies that we are most likely to experience, are not demonic. The spirits we are likely to experience are not mean, not evil, not violent and not poor souls stuck here and in need of release.

Most spirit energies that we experience are from our very own family members or former homeowners. They are guiding us and protecting us. They are helpful and loving.

I also hope to enable "everyday people" to accept the spirit influence in their lives. You might be surprised by the number of people who will open up about some incident in their lives when you express your openness to a rational view of the paranormal. How many more people avoid any discussion of their *personal* paranormal experiences for fear of ridicule or condemnation?

My hope is to bring these issues to light and add a positive aspect to our popular beliefs. I want to encourage people to think about the potential in their own lives. Each of us deserves the opportunity to enjoy and to be enjoyed by our loved ones--even after they pass from this life.

Enjoy!

Sydney Sherman

Acknowledgements

To all those who assisted in this work through their cooperation and support, I offer my thanks.

The subjects of my case histories and the participants in my survey are among the many without whom this book would not be possible.

Those willing to explore the potential of the afterlife continue to encourage me with their curiosity and openness. The commitment of the ghost-hunting community sustains my dedication to demystifying this subject.

I would also like to acknowledge the internet resources cited in the text for making supporting information readily available.

Dedication

To my loving husband and two wonderful sons who are the inspiration for all that I do. Your love, caring and support made this book possible.

To my parents for teaching me the virtues of Honesty and Respect and for loving me despite my difference.

And finally, to all my friends who have supported and encouraged me to keep going. Thank you for knowing how important it was for me to do this.

My Grandfather Cleo Sherman Fitch

Grandma Philomena Helen Celia

Chapter 1 Who Am I ?

My journey from where I began to who I am today is a complicated one. I was born in the 1960s, raised by a mother and a father with brothers and sisters all in a small, rural town in Connecticut.

My father worked; my mother stayed home to raise the children. We went to Catholic Mass and had family dinners on Sunday. We sat through many baseball games and piano recitals. Nothing strange about that. Pretty normal for those times. That's how things were.

I was a normal child, the youngest. I liked to sing, play piano and crochet. Again, pretty normal. I was an everyday child–just like everyone else.

Well, not really.

Imagine how that everyday child is transformed. One day you are like everyone else. With the next day comes the realization that you are different; you have a secret. A secret that can cause you joy, pain, anger or resentment all at the same time. The type of secret that some people will accept, while others condemn. A secret that can cause a family embarrassment and a child shame.

I see dead people. That's it. That was my secret. They're always around me; I am truly never alone. Lonely people pray for someone to talk to. I used to pray for quiet. For me, silence is deafening.

As a child, there were not a lot of people around (at least the ones you see) with whom I could share my secret. Especially not back then. Children were seen and not heard. Everyone was trying to be like the Cleavers–to be just like everyone else. It was a different time. I can't say I *felt* different. I looked like everyone else. I had a good life; I had what I needed. But I **was** different.

The worst part about my secret was how I found I had one.

In first grade I remember standing outside in line waiting to be brought into school. I was talking to my school friend, when another little girl approached. I didn't know who she was, but she seemed to enjoy standing with us. I asked, "What's your name?" My schoolmate asked me who I was talking to. I stated her name and pointed. To my friend I was pointing at thin air. My friend started laughing at me and said *"You're stupid, there's nobody there."* Of course, she **was** there. I **saw** her. As the taunts continued, I started to cry and ran all the way home.

As I ran home, I remember thinking *"She's the one who is stupid if she can't see her!"* *"I **know** she was there".* From then on, I didn't want anyone in school to know about the girl. I didn't want my friend to laugh at me anymore. I continued to see the little girl at school and others as well, but refrained from talking to them. *"That's how it has to be."* I thought.

As time went on, more and more similar experiences occurred. I was made fun of, laughed at. I finally realized that I had something wrong with me. That I was different. I didn't like it. Some call it a gift. This was a gift I wanted to return. I could not understand how they could **not** see them or feel them as I could.

As I got into my teen years, I became able to see that **everyone** had people around them **all** the time. Not people like you or me, but they were there just the same. My ability to hear, see and smell them became more apparent as well. They would reach out and touch me. I can feel them and they can feel me. I would watch the facial expressions of others while "their people" stood with them and tried to speak to them, or touch them. There was no acknowledgement or sense of recognition on their faces.

Sometimes I felt alone. Even when surrounded by spirits, I often wished to be alone. I **prayed** to be alone. I wanted to be normal. Why couldn't I be like everyone else? What was wrong with me?

Finally, tired and confused, I began listening to my spirits. After pushing them away for so long, they talked to me; I listened. They guided me; I followed. I began to understand that there was nothing wrong with me.

Yes, I was different, but no **so** much. I had the ability to see and hear things others could not. Some people compose great music while others write great novels and some have voices like angels. So, although my ability was out-of-the-ordinary, I was not **that** much different. I felt better about myself.

I didn't know what to call these people, but soon found myself calling them "*peeps*". I began using other names to describe the types of personalities I witnessed. There were "*yettetahs*"; this is someone who talks a lot. "*Goobers*" like to play pranks and joke, and a "*Whisperer*", (Well, what do you think?) that's for a quiet talker or one who rarely talks.

They (the peeps) would tell stories, ask questions or just watch the people they were with. Sometimes they would ask me to tell their people things. I wanted to; sometimes I even tried to, but I held myself back once again. I was still afraid; just like the little girl at school who was laughed at for seeing people who "weren't there".

I have my peeps with me all the time. I know them to be family members now. My peeps lived in the past. There are some I never met while they were "alive". Some of my "peeps" lived long before I was born.

That's how it is. Your loved ones are there. Which ones, I don't know. How they find us, I don't know. We can't pick them, but each brings us an energy that we need. They are our guardian angels. They didn't scare me. To me, they were just like the rest of us.

Not long after I finally accepted my gift, I would have to deal with something a little too close to home. Something that was going to change my appreciation for what I can give others in a very unique way. Up to this point, I had not had to deal with the death of a close loved one. That was about to change.

When my grandmother died, I was 16. I loved my grandmother. But she hadn't been "my grandma" for a long time. She had forgotten who she was. She had forgotten who we, her family, were. Alzheimer's had made sure of that. Even though I had been used to seeing people who had passed, I didn't want to see her. I didn't want to believe she would be anyplace else but here with us. My grandma was the first member of my family—someone close to me--who passed. I wasn't ready for this.

I remember my mother as she faced the loss. As an only child without siblings, the loss hit her hard.

My father was Mom's strength in dealing with Grandma's passing. And for the first time to me, my mother looked old, sad.

The evening after my grandmother's funeral, I was in my room sitting on my bed and I smelled my grandma. I could smell her *Just as if she was standing next to me.*

I was scared. I closed my eyes; I didn't want to see her. When I opened my eyes, there she stood at the foot of my bed.

She is beautiful. She is young. Smiling and happy. There is no more "lost gaze" or arthritic fingers. I can see every detail from the dark curls of her hair to her sharp, crooked nose. It was **my** grandma. Not the grandmother that left, but the Grandma I remembered. I cried. She said one thing to me *"I'm not sick anymore."* I smiled. She wasn't sick anymore, she was fine.

That is not to say that it erased my grief. I would rather have loved ones fully present as living, breathing individuals. I still grieve when someone close to me passes, but the loss is not as deep or enduring. I have the knowledge they will be with me if and when I need them.

My Grandma was and is just like all the others I've seen over the years. All happy, full, whole. What was there to be so sad about?

How fortunate I was to experience this! And I want others to experience their loved ones as well. I wanted my mother, hurting so deeply with her loss, to understand; to recognize that death is not a permanent loss. This is a new experience, a new relationship.

My mother is not a believer. Some people, even in the face of their own personal experiences, have a hard time believing. And why should they believe? Would I be a believer if I did not know what I know?

Despite the way we close ourselves to our own "peeps", as a society we seem to have a strong desire to *believe*, at least in some intellectual fashion. Unlike my mother, many of us are willing to believe **something**. We are willing to consider there is more beyond the familiar and commonplace even though we really don't know anything about it. However, the unfamiliar is often more comfortable at arms length.

Many people will tell you they do not believe. However, more people have an expectation of some kind of continuation of this life. They may not know what the other life is, but they believe. And, most people have a general desire to believe that we have, not only the ability to live on, but that we have the ability to maintain some kind of relationship with the living or to reconnect with those from the past.

We will discuss different philosophies, cultures, and customs, encountered in the practice of communicating with the dead. I want to share with you some experiences I've had with spirits. And, with their permission, give you a glimpse into some readings for other people and how their lives were touched through this connection.

All of us at one time will find ourselves facing the end of this existence. Regardless of our gender, nationality, religion or personal beliefs, we all share the same future eventually. All of us must experience the end of our own lives and of those close to us. Most people who prepare for anything ensure themselves a smooth transition. This is also true of our journey at the end of this life.

It is an important opportunity. You have the ability to prepare yourself **and** your family and the ones you love for the process of communication.

We **can** still have a relationship with those who have passed; not the same relationship, different, but still a relationship. And so I begin.

Chapter 2 How Important Could It Be ?

Chapter 2 How Important Could It Be?

In 1981 I gained new insight into the importance of "peeps" in our lives. While the names have been changed, the events below are entirely factual.

As I explained, I've always been aware of "peeps"–the presence of spirits of those who once lived. I see them, hear them, feel them, and even smell them. After being the subject of ridicule as a very young child, I had learned to keep all this to myself.

With the 1970's upsurge of horror films, I was even more aware of my difference. The portrayal of these spirits was all wrong. Dead "peeps" don't look like that, and they certainly aren't here to harm us or eat our flesh. Still, I felt the need to keep my secret to myself.

In High School, only two close friends knew of my ability. They never criticized me or questioned what I do. However, I did not dream of sharing my secret with anyone else.

This was all about to change.

In college, I became friends with a fellow nursing student. We'll call her "Lucy". Neither one of us had any idea how soon our lives would change; all because of her dead Grandma.

"Dotty" was Grandma's name. I had never heard my friend talk about her; however, "Dotty" was always there. Usually quiet and reserved, at one point "Dotty" grew increasingly agitated and loud. This was not her usual self. Dotty's statements were always the same "*White car*" and "*Row of trees*". What??? A little more information would be helpful, but for now that was not to be.

After it was obvious that "Dotty" was not going to stop, I decided to share my secret with Lucy. She was less then interested. Lucy stated *"Yeah, but will she help me find where my family jewels are hidden?"* I told her that I was serious and needed her help. She declined. Nonetheless, "Dotty", persisted.

"Dotty" soon came to realize that if I was going to help her, she needed to help me. In addition to the words, I began picturing a long vacant country road. Then a row of tall trees on the right side came to my mind. I saw a small white car driving down the road, then nothing. Again, I sought Lucy's help with this scenario. Lucy had a small black Honda, not a white car. It didn't make any sense. Again, Lucy was no help offering *"Don't give up your day job."*

Dotty's agitation and insistence continued for about 3 more days. Clearly, this was so important to Dotty that she would not leave me alone. Early on the morning of the 4th day, while on my way to school, I was sitting at a traffic light when another picture formed in my head. It was Lucy getting into a small white car and an African American man handing her the keys. There was a sign above his head that said "OORE" with a star above the double "OO". In the vision in my head, Lucy drove away, passed a Dairy Queen and turned onto a side road, with a signpost containing "CR 14". I couldn't see the rest. Then the scene repeated the same long road with the tall trees

I still didn't know what all this meant. I did know that something very serious was about to happen.

When I got to school, Lucy was not there. I called her house and her father told me her mother had brought her to town to get a rental car. I asked him where and he stated *"Moore's Auto"*. I immediately left school for town and found Moore's Auto.

There was Lucy getting into a small white Corolla and an African American man standing next to the car handing her the keys. Above his head was the sign "Moore's Auto" with a star above the "OO"

My heart sank like a lead weight into my stomach. I ran screaming and yelling for Lucy to get out of the car. I pleaded. I begged. I promised things that I knew I couldn't deliver. I was determined to do whatever it took to keep her out of that rental car.

It worked. Lucy listened to me. She got into my car and commented *"You need to be locked up"*. All I could say was *"Yeah, probably"*. I didn't care; I had her in my car. It was over. We drove away and Dotty was finally quiet.

The next day I went to pick up Lucy for school--one of my many promises. She got into my car. She looked pale, frozen. I asked her *"What's wrong?"* She told me *"Yesterday, a telephone pole caught fire from a transformer and fell on a car, killing a pregnant woman inside instantly."* She looked at me and stated *"I was supposed to be on that road!"* I sat there. I couldn't think. I couldn't do anything.

At this point, I told Lucy I needed to see this road. She directed me to a side road--CR142 (Sound familiar?). In front of me was a long country road. As I continued to drive, I saw a long row of trees on the right side of the road and then the obvious signs of the accident the day before. I couldn't do anything but cry.

This incident changed me. It took me a long time to come to terms with what had happened. As happy as I was with having my friend with me, I couldn't get over the fact that someone still died that day. Two people died that day. By saving my friend did I somehow cause the death of a young pregnant mother? The good that came for one family, was overwhelming grief for another. This was not a gift.

This was a dramatic example of the responsibility I might bear with this "gift". I have come to terms with the double-sided nature of my ability. I've also accepted that it is not my job to edit what I hear and see. My task is to offer my observations as I receive them.

As the years went on I continued to have experiences. I soon realized these "peeps" were always going to be with me. There is nothing I can do about it except, I hope, help others understand that there is no ending after our physical bodies no longer hold us. We move on, yes, but we don't move away. We still see, hear and, if allowed, we can comfort and protect the ones we love.

As for me, I've decided that just as some are given the gift of music or writing great literature, I've been given a gift... sometimes an annoying gift, but still a gift.

All I ask is that you open your ears, unlock all your senses, and allow your "peeps" to be a part of your life.

As for those of you who feel that I need to be "locked up", I say "Yeah, probably".

Chapter 3 Through My Eyes... What Do I Experience ?

One of the first things I tell people is that everything they have been told, read about, or watched on TV about the afterlife is probably **not** true. Or at least, not based upon science.

We, the living, are not even 100% sure what happens to us when we die. Even I don't know what, exactly, happens to us when we leave this life. While we can gain some insights, the "big picture" is left to speculation.

Just the name "afterlife" is not appropriate. What is life? The word life has different interpretations for different people. We have all heard the arguments on both sides, in the courts, legislation and within various religions, of when life begins. And with each one of these, their definition of life differs.

To know when life begins is to know the very nature of life. Is life based upon the first breath we ever take? Is life a means by which we exist? Is it at the cellular level? Is it after conception? You can look in many dictionaries for the word life and get many different definitions all based on fact, presumption or science.

Some people describe life not by the beginning of one's existence, but by how one **lives** that life. My work is concerned with what we get out of life as a result of what we put into our lives.

When does life start; when does it cease? Is it the loss of what others know us to be from our physical appearance or the loss of who we truly are? We know life as change. I do not think that life ends the changes. Let me explain.

I believe you can't look at life as if it meets any of the standard descriptions without keeping in mind one very important fact. We are energy. That is a fact. There are no uncertainties about this. Creationists, biblical scholars, physicists and even Big Bang theorists do not argue that we are energy. And they agree that this energy has been in existence since the beginning of time. Now what you believe about how this energy was created is a personal one based upon your values, beliefs and feelings. But regardless of the different theories of its inception, all theories agree about the constancy of energy.

One of the basic laws of science is the "law of conservation of energy". This law simply states that energy can neither be created nor destroyed. It can only be changed from one form to another.

There is no doubt we are energy. Everything that makes us who we are requires energy. It is our life force. So once we have completed this lifecycle, our energy continues on.

Is this an argument therefore for reincarnation? Some would think so. And some would say (including me) that there is certainly an argument for this.

So let's continue with this theory. Our bodies, our flesh and bones are the apparatus which houses who we truly are. Our bodies keep us warm; they protect us. They are an identifier, a means of mutual recognition. Everything that makes us who we are, our personality, our feelings, comes from deep within us, not from outward appearances.

When we pass, our energy still exists. We are still here. However our physical bodies can no longer survive. Whether it be by injury or through disease or aging, the physical body ceases to function.

So there is a separation of our physical form from our life force. The fragility and deterioration of our physical bodies are no longer a burden to the energy. Our illnesses or diseases or other malformations no longer exist. These were all outward, physical flaws; we have been separated from all that. Therefore, that which is left is a whole being; a complete energy.

You will notice that I usually choose not to use words such as death or ghosts. I choose to use words more descriptive of what I have seen and experienced. We pass from one arena to another. There is no death. The term "death" for most signifies the ceasing of one's ability to be a viable energy -- a completion and end. I say that is not so. And hopefully, after you've read this book, you will understand why I'm so firm in my beliefs. Hopefully, you will have a better understanding of our energies.

As I said before, I also choose not to use the word ghosts. The word ghosts, by context, is a very demeaning term invoked by TV, movies and books. Our spirit, our energy is a more appropriate description and certainly more accurate. Now let's discuss why I believe as I do.

People ask me *"What do you see?"* I tell them *"It varies"*. I see different effects in different situations. I can see full figures, shadows, energy fields, light anomalies or sometimes, nothing at all. But, there's always a sense of the person near me.

I can also smell the energies. Sometimes I can only hear them. I do not know why my sense is different for some spirits. As I have explained to many people over the years, I don't have the answers to everything. I myself still have many questions I would like answered.

I will say that most spirits will present in a physical form which would be recognizable for us. They are always younger. They have told me that they can be what ever age they wish, usually when they were the most happy.

What I find truly amazing is the choices these spirits make. Most people would assume that they will come back in their 20s when they had less responsibility, maybe not so many worries or aches and pains. However, many appear a bit older. I would say the majority present in their early to mid 30s.

If a person has passed as a young child, they present at the age of their passing, usually having an older relative as a guide. There is one thing for sure; age has no meaning to them in any other way. Age is-irrelevant to them--completely independent of time. Perhaps presenting this way keeps them connected to this life? Perhaps they hope the visible presentation they select will be more acceptable to us.

What is least anticipated about our "peeps"? The one thing that most people are fascinated to hear is that the personality and behavior one had in this life is the same now as it was when they were "alive". Personality does not change. You will not find all your "peeps" acting like perfect angels. If their behavior was that of a doting mother, they will present as such. If they were mean, self-centered jerks; sorry, they are still jerks.

Why is that? Because that is who we are. That is our recognizable energy. The perception that all people who pass float around wearing white flowing clothing with wings or playing a harp on a cloud, speaking of only happy things is a fantasy. I'm sorry to say all those preconceived notions of what it is like to be dead are not true. The angel-like presentation of those who have passed is fueled by popular media, but, not based in any reality.

It is also not true that they throw items around or cause walls to bleed. Can they move items? Yes. Can they manipulate the environment? Yes. But please keep in mind that the majority of these entities are our loved ones. Their intention is not to cause harm or to even scare us. Their actions are an attempt to get our attention.

I'm sure most of us have seen episodes of shows like *The Twilight Zone.* You're walking down a crowded street or through hallways filled with people. They don't see you. They don't hear you. You become more frustrated, upset and frightened. You begin doing anything you can to get their attention. I imagine it is similar for those who have passed. To be noticed is a desire for all of us. It is no different for our "peeps".

Through my eyes I see healthy, vibrant energy, not decaying corpses or zombies. Mothers, fathers, sisters, brothers, husbands, wives and even children. All whole, all happy. I've never experienced anything different.

They will move jewelry, open cabinets, knock pictures down. But all these things are done with a desire to be noticed. And I expect you would do the same.

When people report the presence of evil "demons" in their home and describe physical events, I ask them "How *were you hurt?*" "*How bad was the damage?*" The answer is always the same. No harm was done; nothing was damaged. If we are guided by the images we gather from TV and movies, it is easy to misinterpret the events and ignore the obvious. If the activity was truly demonic or malevolent, there would be no question in anyone's mind of what they had experienced. The thought that only something wicked with evil intent can manipulate these things is false. But again, most of what we know is based on popular media derived from folklore and legend.

People are always amazed when I give them reading. They expect something much different than what they get. They expect pat answers. I am not just going to tell you that grandma or grandpa is okay and that they love you. Of course they are, and of course they do. These are not the type of conversations they have, nor is it the information that you are looking for.

However, what **you** think is important, may not necessarily be what is important to **them.** Your memories and their memories may differ. The focus is on what's important to **them.**

In most conversations they offer what I call "validation statements"--information that in the grand scheme of life doesn't mean a lot to most, but **will** be meaningful to you.

Often, they tell you of things that are occurring in your life right now; people you've seen, places you've gone, things you are doing. These are all a corroboration of their identity. They need to demonstrate that they are with you every day and very much part of your life.

Your spirits talk as if they were sitting on the couch next to you having a conversation. They can make comments about their dislike of your new hair color or even the extra pounds you put around your middle. They don't miss anything. It is very real because they are very real.

When people first experience contact, they have mixed emotions. The expectation conflicts with the reality of the encounter. I attempt to help my clients understand the interactions. What better way to verify that their energies continue to be in your life? Your "peeps" already share your experiences with you; they reveal the things that are going on in your everyday life to confirm their continuing connection to you.

My readings are always very long. And education is always the key. I want my clients to take away with them a new understanding of what lies ahead. After all, one day we will all have the opportunity to experience this new life.

I have been asked many times whether I believe in heaven or hell. Being raised Catholic we were taught the lessons of being good to ourselves and others. We were warned that the choices we make in this life influence where we will spend the rest of eternity. We can either enjoy our new life in heaven where we can live forever, or suffer the flames of eternal damnation in hell where we will suffer pain and torture for all eternity.

My experiences lead me to believe our place in the "afterlife" is not that cut and dried. I can only tell you what I know to be true. I can only share **my** experiences. You will have to make your own determination.

What I see is that everyone, regardless of how they lived their life on this Earth, is together in the same place. They do not speak of a heaven or hell. There does not appear to be a division amongst them. Rich or poor, black or white, all are the same. Again, I do not wish to offend your beliefs and cultural traditions. I can again only express to you my own experience.

In the Catholic Church, as in other religions, to commit suicide is against the will of God and therefore preclusion to the entrance to Heaven. I have given many readings to many people who have had relatives who passed due to suicide. Whether the means of death was suicide, accident or old age, they appear the same; there is no distinction or difference between them. This is comforting to loved ones who struggle with the judgments brought fourth by faith or society.

I do believe in a higher power and in our obligation to do what is morally right by each other. I also believe that we have been given this great opportunity to enjoy family and friends beyond the loss of our physical selves. We should not lose sight of the extraordinary possibilities of extending our relationships beyond death. Life is good and the bonds we make here make us stronger and carry over to guide us in the next life.

My ability to share relationships not only with the living, but with their loved ones who have passed, means a great deal to me. I take it very seriously.

I never forget, not for one day, that I am dealing with people's emotions--sometimes very raw emotions. The delicate nature of this topic in itself can be distressful to some. My hope is that people who read this and share this with their family and friends will understand there does not need to be an end. There does not need to be a conclusion to a relationship. As the old saying goes, life goes on...I'm here to tell you my friend it truly does.

Chapter 3 Through My Eyes… What Do I Experience ?

Chapter 4 Myths About Life After Death...
Sorting Out the Significance

When you "come out" about a gift like mine, even to just a few close friends and family, you may be subject to ridicule, disbelief and even condemnation.

Part of the process of examining my gift and what it meant for me included questions like. *'Was I playing God?"*, *"Did my information save one person and contribute to the death of others?".* I also needed to address the other taunts I had faced. *"You're a demon"*, *"You are playing with the Devil"*, *"All ghosts are evil forces trying to deceive us."* And the like.

Now, I was brought up in a good Catholic family, so I want you to know this was a serious consideration and I spent a lot of time searching the Bible, religious quotations and other references regarding "Ghosts" and spirits of various sorts.

What do we really know about all these beings? Have people believed in these ideas for centuries? Do they believe the same in other cultures? Some of the answers are surprising.

This chapter is to share some of the references to different kinds of spirits or beings and my own speculations as to why they appear in our culture.

I believe it is worth noting that many of the terms we expect to be static, universal definitions have changed considerably over the centuries and across different religions or cultures. It certainly suggests that we look at the context of time and culture when we read about these beings.

As far back as we have been in existence, we as a culture have believed in the existence of strange and inexplicable things. Werewolves, witches, Bigfoot, the Bermuda Triangle etc. Some such legends appeared generations, hundreds and even thousands of years ago. Others are of recent origin. It is likely the claims were perpetuated for different reasons. We, as a society, have a desire to know. What we don't know, we sometimes make up. We will discuss just a few myths now and what we know of their origins.

Not only do our ideas on inexplicable things change, merge and evolve as they are translated into another language or culture. The treatment of these entities in popular culture has also affected our beliefs.

Some myths involve legendary creatures. They do not concern spirits.

Examples include Bigfoot, a larger than human ape-like creature, and Werewolves. This type of myth has little to offer the topic of ghosts, but gives us some insight into the lure of the unusual. Since ancient times, humans have been attracted to tales of fantastic or legendary creatures.

BIGFOOT

Historically, the first Bigfoot-like creature we see is the Yeti or Abominable Snowman. These creatures were said to live in the Himalayan region of Nepal, and Tibet. Although we can speculate the myth was originated hundreds or even thousands of years ago, they probably do not reach back as far as Gigantopithecus, a large ape up to 10' tall who was reported to have roamed the forest of Asia around 300,000 years ago and walked on two feet. Anthropologists theorize "Fossil remains of Gigantopithecus could have led to the myth of the Yeti, and some fringe researchers believe it's possible populations of the creature may have persisted into recent times, giving root to the Bigfoot legend." [1]

However, it was only in the 19th century that such creatures appeared in western popular culture. Stories and even pictures and video from the Pacific Northwest appear as "proof" of the existence of Bigfoot A.K.A. Sasquatch.

Within scientific circles, Bigfoot sightings are usually classified as hoaxes or considered a misidentification of some known animal. [2] [3]

WEREWOLVES

A werewolf, also known as a lycanthrope, is a human with the ability to shape shift into a wolf or wolf-like creature. They are generally believed to be humans who undergo a transformation rather than a spiritual being or a once-living human, but there are some exceptions. According to legend, the cause could be a curse or a bite from another werewolf... often on a full moon. [4]

Our fascination with transformation into wolves reaches far back into history. It is documented as early as second century B.C. Greece. Later references came from locations as distant as Sweden, Serbia, Asia and Haiti.

1 "Yeti." *Wikipedia: The Free Encyclopedia.* Wikimedia Foundation, Inc. 24 March 2012. Web. 24 March 2012. <http://en.wikipedia.org/wiki/Yeti>
2 "Yeti." *Wikipedia: The Free Encyclopedia.* Wikimedia Foundation, Inc. 24 March 2012. Web. 24 March 2012. <http://en.wikipedia.org/wiki/Yeti>
3 "Bigfoot." *Wikipedia: The Free Encyclopedia.* Wikimedia Foundation, Inc. 24 March 2012. Web. 24 March 2012. <http://en.wikipedia.org/wiki/Bigfoot>
4 "Werewolf." *Wikipedia: The Free Encyclopedia.* Wikimedia Foundation, Inc. 24 March 2012. Web. 24 March 2012. <http://en.wikipedia.org/wiki/Werewolf>

How do you recognize a werewolf in human form? According to European folklore, you look for the meeting of the eyebrows, curved fingernails, low-set ears and a swinging stride.[5]

We can only speculate on the imagination that brought us our common image of werewolves. However, if you combine a fear of wolves with some knowledge of excessively hairy people; add some superstitions about humans being transformed into something "not human"; you might just get a werewolf.

Up until the 20th century, wolves were not uncommon in rural areas and, "wolf attacks on humans were an occasional, but widespread feature of life in Europe... Some scholars have suggested that it was inevitable that wolves, being the most feared predators in Europe, were projected into the folklore of evil shape shifters." [6]

One of the reported tales that added to the hysteria was of a boy in a small village who developed facial hair as well as long hairs on his arms, back and legs. With an age well before puberty, clearly something was seriously wrong with him. Why would he look like a wolf? Hence the story to of a young boy, bitten by a wolf when the moon was full, who was transformed into this horrible creature. The night would be his. He would hunt prey at night and, as with the vampires, his victims would also take on his curse and

---

5 "Werewolf:Classical Literature." *Wikipedia: The Free Encyclopedia*. Wikimedia Foundation, Inc. 24 March 2012. Web. 24 March 2012.
<http://en.wikipedia.org/wiki/Werewolf#Classical_literature>
6 "Werewolf." *Wikipedia: The Free Encyclopedia*. Wikimedia Foundation, Inc. 24 March 2012. Web. 24 March 2012. <http://en.wikipedia.org/wiki/Werewolf>

become werewolves. This story caused panic and unrest. A hunting frenzy ensued with the killing of many poor innocent wolves. Our myths could have evolved from a scenario like the one above.

Frequently we respond to the different or unknown with fear and suspicion rather than rational thought. Now this boy (if he truly existed) was probably suffering from hypertrichosis or a variant disease called Hirtuism (It is reported some sufferers were so visibly hairy, they became circus sideshow performers in the 19th and early 20th centuries.) He was different. He was not a wolf-boy as some would say. But sometimes it's easier to believe than not.[7]

In various settings and eras, our traditions and myths are intertwined with spiritual beliefs. Some of our myths have to do with entities that are mostly spiritual beings but may have some other interrelationship with mythical beings.

The phrases Demon, Devil and Witch might seem clear cut terms, but, over the centuries have taken on different characteristics. Let's start with demons.

DEMONS

A demon (or daemon) is "a supernatural being found in numerous religions, occultisms, literatures and folklores. A demon is sometimes defined as an evil spirit or devil."[8]

---

7 "Hypertrichosis." *Wikipedia: The Free Encyclopedia.* Wikimedia Foundation, Inc. 24 March 2012. Web. 24 March 2012. <http://en.wikipedia.org/wiki/Hypertrichosis>
8 "Demon." *Wikipedia: The Free Encyclopedia.* Wikimedia Foundation, Inc. 24 March 2012. Web. 24 March 2012. <http://en.wikipedia.org/wiki/Demon>

Typically, a demon is malevolent and not a human entity. They are sometimes described as unclean spirits and thought to be the cause of "demonic possessions". The concept of a demon plays on our fears of something "taking over", overcoming our own spirits with evil.

Very early, pre-Christian references like the Greek considered them spiritual beings, but not necessarily evil. "In Greek culture, daimones originally meant "divine beings... god-like, ministering spirits, protective spirits" or in "Plato... middle-ranking creatures of the air, interacting between gods and mankind." or even (in Socrates) "guardian spirits that everyone has, but also as the inner voice that guided him in choosing to do right, rather than wrong."[9]

But they could also be the spirits of the dead *"daimones were at times the spirits of the dead, or ghosts, who could be sought for advice; and that the daimones were also messengers similar to the modern beliefs in angels"*.[10]

Some believe leaders of the early Christian Church attacked the demons to distinguish and discredit ancient Greek and other beliefs from those of Christianity. After the rise of Christianity, demons are usually an evil spirit that may come from the netherworld, be a fallen angel who rebelled against God or the evil spawn of fallen angels and human women. Reference to demons or demon-like spirits is found in

---

9 "Demon." *Wikipedia: The Free Encyclopedia.* Wikimedia Foundation, Inc. 24 March 2012. Web. 24 March 2012. <http://en.wikipedia.org/wiki/Demon>

10 "Demon." *Wikipedia: The Free Encyclopedia.* Wikimedia Foundation, Inc. 24 March 2012. Web. 24 March 2012. <http://en.wikipedia.org/wiki/Demon>

Mesopotamia, Ancient Arabia, the Hebrew Bible, Christianity, Islam and Hinduism among other traditions.[11]

"Some religions and traditions... identify these names [various demons] as guises of The Devil. Even when thought of as individual demons, some are often thought of being under the Devil's direct control"[12]

Some still believe demons are wicked agents of the devil who are out to get humanity.

While there are a few traditions that have no defined idea of "The Devil", in many religions and cultures, "The Devil" is believed to be a powerful, supernatural entity that is the **personification of evil** and the enemy of God and humankind.

Other concepts include: the "Chief Adversary of God" that wars for human souls, a tempter, a fallen angel, a demon or the Chief of all demons.

Some emphasize pure evil and evil intent, for others the Devil is an agent of testing, tempting or tricking humans. And, more recently, some consider references to the Devil as a more allegorical representation of an internal human battle between the good and the lower natures of humans.

"Christian tradition has frequently identified pagan religions and witchcraft with the influence of Satan. In the Early Modern

11 "Demon." *Wikipedia: The Free Encyclopedia.* Wikimedia Foundation, Inc. 24 March 2012. Web. 24 March 2012. <http://en.wikipedia.org/wiki/Demon>
12 "Devil." *Wikipedia: The Free Encyclopedia.* Wikimedia Foundation, Inc. 24 March 2012. Web. 24 March 2012. <http://en.wikipedia.org/wiki/Devil>

Period, the Church accused alleged witches of consorting and conspiring with Satan." [13]

The Bible and Biblical scholars for centuries have told stories about such evil i.e., the devil, Lucifer, a fallen angel, under whose sway, the souls of sinners are condemned to the fiery pits of hell. The Bible clearly describes an angel of God who became jealous and wanted all that God had for himself. He turned his back on God and was cast out of the Kingdom of Heaven. He was evil and responsible for all things bad. A person with an unholy heart was said to have opened himself up to the Devil.

Religious education teaches us that those who were good and followed the teachings of God *"shall enter his kingdom"*. Now I'm not saying that **all** this is a myth, there's compelling evidence to suggest the continued combat occurs daily between good versus evil.

Some say that I am not really communicating with loved ones of my clients, but with Satan or some other demon disguised as loving family members, who, by the way, provide helpful, protective and comforting information to the living. This is ridiculous as far as I'm concerned. A little later on, we'll take a look at issues of misreading and misinterpretation of Biblical passages on spirits.

---

13 "Devil." *Wikipedia: The Free Encyclopedia.* Wikimedia Foundation, Inc. 24 March 2012. Web. 24 March 2012. <http://en.wikipedia.org/wiki/Devil>

WITCHES

Another example of changing characterizations is the witch. The definitions and views of witches have had an evolving and imprecise history as well.

Witches are commonly thought to be people who worship the devil or cast spells. These spells can cause pain and sickness or death. Some might wonder why I include witchcraft in this discussion. Everyone knows there truly are and have been cultures that have practiced the dark arts, conjured up spirits, and placed spells on those who angered them. And yes, they even perform animal sacrifice. We also know the accusation of witchcraft was frequently unjustified. The confusion of myth with religion resulted in widespread fear and both death and hardship for innocent people.

The term witch (from Old English) was **not always** exclusively evil. A variety of terms were used interchangeably for male or female healers we might consider "white witches". These witches, sometimes termed "practitioners, 'white', 'good', or 'unbinding' witches, blessers, wizards, sorcerers, "cunning-men" or "wise-men", "may have considered themselves the mediators between humans" and the spiritual worlds."[14]

In pre-Christian cultures, the word "witch" did not exist, but there is widespread reference to sorcery and written

---

14 "Witchcraft:Demonology." *Wikipedia: The Free Encyclopedia.* Wikimedia Foundation, Inc. 24 March 2012. Web. 24 March 2012. <http://en.wikipedia.org/wiki/Witchcraft#Demonology>

reference to *"unjustified spells"* found as early as the Babylonian code of Hammurabi (~ 1775 BC).[15]

In particular, *"within Christianity and Islam, sorcery came to be associated with evil and heresy. Witches were thought to be part of the Devil's secret army in opposition to God."* [16]

Between the fifteenth and eighteenth centuries (the "Early Modern period"), was an era of witch hunts across Europe, and to some extent the European colonies in North America. There was widespread hysteria that satanic witches were operating as an organized threat to Christendom.

Those accused of witchcraft were portrayed as worshippers of the Devil, who engaged in sorcery and orgies at meetings known as Witches' Sabbaths. Once accused of witchcraft, men and women were put on trial for the crime. The severity of punishment differed according to the location and the period. The witch trials originated in south-eastern France during the fourteenth century, before spreading through central Europe and then into other parts of the continent. The fear also spread to European colonies in North America. While early trials fall still within the Late Medieval period, the peak of the witch hunting was between 1580 and 1630.

Interpretations of biblical passages such as *"Deuteronomy 18:11-12 condemns anyone who "casts spells, or who is a medium or spiritist or who consults the dead. Anyone who*

---

15 "Witchcraft:Ancient Near East." *Wikipedia: The Free Encyclopedia.* Wikimedia Foundation, Inc. 24 March 2012. Web. 24 March 2012.
2012,<http://en.wikipedia.org/wiki/Witchcraft#Ancient_Near_East>
16 "Witchcraft:Demonology." *Wikipedia: The Free Encyclopedia.* Wikimedia Foundation, Inc. 24 March 2012. Web. 24 March 2012. <http://en.wikipedia.org/wiki/Witchcraft#Demonology>

- 32 -

does these things is detestable to the Lord, and because of these detestable practices the Lord your God will drive out those nations before you" (NIV); Exodus 22:18 states "Do not allow a sorceress to live" (NIV)."[17] seemed to justify persecution and killing.

Contrary to many assumptions, the Church did not create the idea of witchcraft as a harmful practice requiring a punishment of death.

Elements of medieval attitudes about witchcraft are found in pre-Christian religions. The conception of orgies can be found in Bacchanalias, wild, mystic festivals of the Greco-Roman god Bacchus . At their height ~ 188 BC "nothing (was considered) as impious or criminal" and those who would not fully participate were sacrificed as a victims.[18]

It is hard to imagine any behavior that would be more despicable in the eyes of the Church. It is interesting to note that, for the most part, the witch-hunts did not occur in the "dark" Middle Ages. Most witch hunts take place in "the Early Modern period (about 1480 to 1750), spanning the

---

17 "Christian Views On Magic." Wikipedia: The Free Encyclopedia. Wikimedia Foundation, Inc. 24 March 2012. Web. 24 March 2012.
<http://en.wikipedia.org/wiki/Christian_views_on_magic >
18 "Bacchanalia." Wikipedia: The Free Encyclopedia. Wikimedia Foundation, Inc. 24 March 2012. Web. 24 March 2012. <http://en.wikipedia.org/wiki/Bacchanalia>

upheavals of the Reformation and the Thirty Years' War,"[19] the Renaissance and the Scientific Revolution.[20] [21]

When periods of rapid change, political agitation or prolonged difficult circumstances threaten accustomed ways of life, the resulting frustration and anger may cause communities to seek ready-made scapegoats as their short-cut remedies.[22]

Magical attacks could be an explanation for personal or societal misfortune. Those who were already unusual or at the fringes of society were well-positioned to become scapegoats.

The notion of an undeniable association of sorcery and the Devil is unique to Western witchcraft (Christian and Islamic traditions) after the Early Modern Period. [23]

It appears attitudes began to change around the 9th-11th century and within a few centuries any hint of sorcery was assumed to be in league with the Devil. *"By 1300, the elements were in place for a witch hunt, and for the next*

19 "Witch-hunt." *Wikipedia: The Free Encyclopedia*. Wikimedia Foundation, Inc. 24 March 2012. Web. 24 March 2012. <http://en.wikipedia.org/wiki/Witch-hunt>
20 "Witch-hunt." *Wikipedia: The Free Encyclopedia*. Wikimedia Foundation, Inc. 24 March 2012. Web. 24 March 2012. <http://en.wikipedia.org/wiki/Witch-hunt>
21 "Witchcraft." *Wikipedia: The Free Encyclopedia*. Wikimedia Foundation, Inc. 24 March 2012. Web. 24 March 2012. <http://en.wikipedia.org/wiki/Witchcraft>
22 "Scapegoating." *Wikipedia: The Free Encyclopedia*. Wikimedia Foundation, Inc. 24 March 2012. Web. 24 March 2012. <http://en.wikipedia.org/wiki/ Scapegoating >
23 "Witchcraft." *Wikipedia: The Free Encyclopedia*. Wikimedia Foundation, Inc. 24 March 2012. Web. 24 March 2012. <http://en.wikipedia.org/wiki/ Witchcraft >

century and a half fear of witches spread gradually throughout Europe." [24]

Some suggest the distinguishing factor in later centuries and what switched the responsibility from the Devil to the "witch" was the assumption that *to be a witch, one had to sign a pact with the Devil or worship him--this was heresy and meant damnation.* [25] Selling ones soul, repudiation of Jesus Christ, desecration of the crucifix riding or flying by night, secret nocturnal meetings, stealing, killing or offering babies to the Devil and wild orgies [26] all became commonly accepted beliefs about accused witches.

"At the end of the Middle Ages (about 1450), the fear became a craze which lasted more than 200 years." [27]

Accusations of witchcraft could result from ordinary, but real, difficulties like failed crops and unusual disease or weather. Other suspicions arose from human discord and rivalries. With an atmosphere of suspicion and conspiracy in the public mind, it might be easier to blame an odd neighbor rather than ill fortune.

Witchcraft possessed the element of a conspiracy of the day.

---

24 "Witchcraft." *Wikipedia: The Free Encyclopedia.* Wikimedia Foundation, Inc. 24 March 2012. Web. 24 March 2012. <http://en.wikipedia.org/wiki/European_witchcraft>
25 "European Witchcraft." *Wikipedia: The Free Encyclopedia.* Wikimedia Foundation, Inc. 24 March 2012. Web. 24 March 2012.<http://en.wikipedia.org/wiki/ European_witchcraft >
26 "European Witchcraft." *Wikipedia: The Free Encyclopedia.* Wikimedia Foundation, Inc. 24 March 2012. Web. 24 March 2012. <http://en.wikipedia.org/wiki/ European_witchcraft >
27 "European Witchcraft." *Wikipedia: The Free Encyclopedia.* Wikimedia Foundation, Inc. 24 March 2012. Web. 24 March 2012. <http://en.wikipedia.org/wiki/ European_witchcraft >

Prior to that time one might be accused of maleficium (malevolent sorcery), but it was not automatically associated with Satan and heresy.

The idea of witchcraft as a vast diabolical conspiracy against Christianity was almost certainly pure fiction driven by hysteria. No doubt there was some practice of sorcery intending harm or revenge or even some worship the Devil. However, the charges of flying in the air, changing form into a hare, suckling familiar spirits from warts, or going to sea in an eggshell are strictly fantastic. [28] [29] The fact that accusations were brought against learned people and clergy (even Popes) illustrates the frantic mindset of the time.

The stage was set to mix irrational fear and a persecuting mentality into the emergence of the witch-hunts. Regardless of the time or place, religious authorities and communities under their sway, truly believed in the picture of witches that had been created.[30]

Some common suspicions concerned blighting of crops or livestock, raising storms, causing disease, sexual dysfunction and stillbirths.[31] Witches could also be implicated in disputes and friction surrounding property, inheritance, family feuds, marital discord or difficulties in local politics. If your hen isn't

---

28"European Witchcraft." *Wikipedia: The Free Encyclopedia*. Wikimedia Foundation, Inc. 24 March 2012. Web. 24 March 2012. <http://en.wikipedia.org/wiki/ European_witchcraft >
29 "Witchcraft." *Wikipedia: The Free Encyclopedia*. Wikimedia Foundation, Inc. 24 March 2012. Web. 24 March 2012. <http://en.wikipedia.org/wiki/ Witchcraft >
30 "Witches' Sabbath." *Wikipedia: The Free Encyclopedia*. Wikimedia Foundation, Inc. 24 March 2012. Web. 24 March 2012. <http://en.wikipedia.org/wiki/ Witches'_Sabbath >
31 "European Witchcraft." *Wikipedia: The Free Encyclopedia*. Wikimedia Foundation, Inc. 24 March 2012. Web. 24 March 2012. <http://en.wikipedia.org/wiki/ European_witchcraft >

laying or your cow won't give milk, it might be time to look for a witch.

We've all heard of the Salem witch trials. These witch trials did not only occur in Salem, but through many parts of the Northeast. The hardships and disease that faced colonial New England were rationalized as being caused by the devil. This myth caused so much panic that people began pointing fingers at their neighbors and other family members and accusing them of being involved in witchcraft--the witch-hunt. Even the hint of sorcery triggered a panic mentality. Anyone could be a witch. Soon the suspicion alone could threaten the public order and confidence of an entire community.

With virtually no evidence, these people were hung, burned or stoned to death. A lot of innocent people died. And once one witch was "discovered", panic set in. To a pious, God-fearing community, undeserved, unexplained illness or plagues needed a cause. Bad luck for some was considered a curse brought upon them by devilish practices.

At a time without the knowledge of psychiatric disorders, any out-of-the-ordinary behavior was likely the fault of the Devil.

Some witches had trials. Some did not. Proof was not necessary; getting rid of evil was. Different hypotheses have come to light that suggest some reasons for the strange behavior witnessed by so many in Salem.

Through the summer and into the fall of 1692, twenty-three men and women of Salem, were accused or convicted of witchcraft, most were hung at Gallows Hill, one was stoned and several were pressed to death [32]

The subjects of the odd behaviors were probably not "cursed" or the victims of "souls sold to Satan". They were sick. Historians now speculate that ergot may have led to the Salem witch trials.

When researchers look back to the specific reports at Salem they included delirium, violent convulsions, dashing about, incomprehensible speech and utterance of strange sounds, trance-like states, contorted bodies in frozen postures, and odd skin sensations like pricking, biting and pinching. [33]

"Linda R. Caporael posited in 1976 that the hysterical symptoms of young women that had spurred the Salem witch trials had been the result of consuming ergot-tainted rye." [34] At the time, rye grain was a commonly used for both cereal and bread. Ergot fungus invades developing kernels of rye grain. Damp and rainy summers following cold winters (such as existed prior to the rye harvest in Salem) are known to trigger the ergot infection. Ergotism may cause convulsions, violent fits, burning and crawling sensations on the skin,

---

32 "Timeline of the Salem Witch Trials." *Wikipedia: The Free Encyclopedia.* Wikimedia Foundation, Inc. 24 March 2012. Web. 24 March 2012.
<http://en.wikipedia.org/wiki/Timeline_of_the_Salem_witch_trials>
33 "Salem Witch Trials:Initial Events." *Wikipedia: The Free Encyclopedia.* Wikimedia Foundation, Inc. 24 March 2012. Web. 24 March 2012.
<http://en.wikipedia.org/wiki/Salem_witch_trials#Initial_events>
34 "Ergot." *Wikipedia: The Free Encyclopedia.* Wikimedia Foundation, Inc. 24 March 2012. Web. 24 March 2012. <http://en.wikipedia.org/wiki/Ergot>

vomiting, and hallucinations. (The hallucinogenic drug LSD is a derivative of ergot.) [35]

Perhaps the "bewitched" accusers of Salem had in fact suffered from poisoning by a crop of fungus-infested rye due to wet weather and poor storage conditions. Some indicate many of the accusers lived near wet swampy areas where ergotism would be more likely.

However, ergot poisoning can't explain all of the events at Salem and many have cast doubt on ergotism as the cause of the Salem witch trials. [36]

The timing of the Salem outbreak, just a few years after Cotton Mather's account of the accusation, trial and execution of an Irish washerwoman, for witchcraft in his 1689 "Memorable Providences, Relating to Witchcrafts and Possessions" may be significant. It was reported to be a popular book of the day. [37]

Some of the reactions and behaviors in Salem may have been a result of a mass hysteria--"A common manifestation of mass hysteria occurs when a group of people believe they are suffering from a similar disease or ailment." [38]--suggested by the similarities they had read about.

---

35 "Ergot." *Wikipedia: The Free Encyclopedia.* Wikimedia Foundation, Inc. 24 March 2012. Web. 24 March 2012. <http://en.wikipedia.org/wiki/Ergot>
36 "Ergot." *Wikipedia: The Free Encyclopedia.* Wikimedia Foundation, Inc. 24 March 2012. Web. 24 March 2012. <http://en.wikipedia.org/wiki/Ergot>
37 "Timeline of the Salem Witch Trials." *Wikipedia: The Free Encyclopedia.* Wikimedia Foundation, Inc. 24 March 2012. Web. 24 March 2012.
<http://en.wikipedia.org/wiki/Timeline_of_the_Salem_witch_trials>
38 "Category:Mass Hysteria." *Wikipedia: The Free Encyclopedia.* Wikimedia Foundation, Inc. 24 March 2012. Web. 24 March 2012. <http://en.wikipedia.org/wiki/Category:Mass_hysteria>

Even 40 years earlier, the case of the hanging of "the witch" Goody Knapp in Fairfield, Connecticut Colony suggests the power of community suspicion and peer pressure. There have been no indications of the unusual complaints described in Salem. In 1653 a woman "was executed in (nearby) Stratford after making a confession, probably under torture, which also intimated there were other witches in the area"[39] Goody Knapp was reported to be "a simple-minded woman". [40]

Sources suggest one of the motives behind the charges of witchcraft against her "was to extract from her (Knapp) an accusation against Goody Staples, who had been long suspected of evil doings".

Some believe that single and elderly women were looked upon with suspicion and that they were considered useless to their society.

During Knapp's trial, a midwife was told to examine poor Goody Knapp and found "witch marks" on her. Goody Knapp was found guilty and hanged. However, *"After the body of Goody Knapp was cut down, the women of the town crowded around to see the "witch marks" but found nothing."* [41]

---

39 Eric D Lehman, "A Witch Hanged in Bridgeport," *Bridgeport Library: Bridgeport History Center.* 20. Sep 2011 Web. 24 March 2012. <http://b portlibrary.org/hc/uncategorized/a-witch-hanged-in-bridgeport/>

40 Eric D Lehman, "A Witch Hanged in Bridgeport," *Bridgeport Library: Bridgeport History Center.* 20. Sep 2011 Web. 24 March 2012. <http://b portlibrary.org/hc/uncategorized/a-witch-hanged-in-bridgeport/>

41 Eric D Lehman, "A Witch Hanged in Bridgeport," *Bridgeport Library: Bridgeport History Center.* 20. Sep 2011 Web. 24 March 2012. <http://b portlibrary.org/hc/uncategorized/a-witch-hanged-in-bridgeport/>

Here there is no evidence of any underlying disease. There is blame, suspicion and the pressure of the surrounding community.

Not only are these cautionary tales of the destructive power of suspicion, they are examples of how readily any event or evidence can be replaced by yarns, fictions and myths.

Our views of other entities have undergone comparable transformations over time. Another category to consider is that of myths that assume an afterlife.

What comes after death? There is a natural human curiosity of what happens after our bodies cease to function.

If your point of reference is traditional western religions, you might imagine belief in an afterlife is limited to a few major religions. In fact, a belief in an afterlife--a continued existence of the soul after the death of the body, has been widespread for centuries and most cultures have some belief in an afterlife.

This is generally true whether a religion is based on a God (theistic) or non-theistic (like Buddhism), most believe in some type of afterlife. [42]

In western cultures, "belief in the soul and an afterlife remained near universal until the emergence of atheism in the 18th century." [43]

---

42 "Afterlife." *Wikipedia: The Free Encyclopedia*. Wikimedia Foundation, Inc. 24 March 2012. Web. 24 March 2012. <http://en.wikipedia.org/wiki/Afterlife >
43 "Ghost." *Wikipedia: The Free Encyclopedia*. Wikimedia Foundation, Inc. 24 March 2012. Web. 24 March 2012. < http://en.wikipedia.org/wiki/Ghost>

The next group of myths involves entities that were once alive thereby presuming a life after death.

THE UNDEAD

The undead: ghosts, flesh-eating zombies, poltergeists, incarnates, demons etc, etc., etc. Where did these stories come from?

Undead is the collective name for beings that are deceased yet still display aspects of life. **Animated corpses** could include Mummies, Vampires, Zombies and Ghouls, and Ghosts. Here some element of the human being survives the death of the body and can make itself perceptible to the living. [44]

The pervasive belief in spirits and the afterlife does strengthen the case for the reality of contact with spirits through the ages. Some legends of the undead can be viewed as a confirmation that ancient peoples and diverse cultures had some sense of, belief in, or communication with sprits of those who died.

In some parts of the world, a heritage of belief in spirits almost certainly began with ancestor worship. However, myths, folk tales and cultural beliefs can't be viewed as proof of the reality of **every** paranormal or supernatural being ever reported.

By observing the history and the context of some entities, it is clear some myths serve a personal or cultural purpose.

---

44 "Undead: 19th Century." *Wikipedia: The Free Encyclopedia.* Wikimedia Foundation, Inc. 24 March 2012. Web. 24 March 2012. <http://en.wikipedia.org/wiki/Undead#19th_Century>

The most obvious are the fakes--a fraud who wants to take your money or property, those who want to instill fear, or those attempting to make you dependent in order to take your power or confidence. Later you'll see an example of an attempt to divert unwanted attention from some other situation.

Some myths work for the society or religion. They help a society prevent unwanted behavior, help a group establish a unique identity, help one faction gain or maintain power over another or alleviate fears. They may serve as a way to shift responsibility and find a scapegoat. Some others provide the opportunity for someone to be the "Hero".

But perhaps most basic myths are the ones that address primal fears and offer explanations.

Key targets: fear of not being you (someone/ something taking over), an explanation for some misfortune or affliction, an explanation of the unknown; what happens after we die for instance.

REANIMATED MUMMIES

This myth is pure fantasy and plays on our universal fears.

There is no doubt that careful preservation of mummified bodies (in sometimes elaborate tombs) was practiced in ancient Egypt. However, the combination of a vengeful spirit **with** a wrapped mummy body was **not** known in ancient Egypt. The Mummy, as we know it in popular fiction, probably stems from the many highly publicized late 18th and early 19th century archeological discoveries in Egypt. Egyptian history captured the popular imagination. That imagination gave birth to the disturbed spirit wreaking vengeance--"The Mummy" of modern popular fiction.

An 1827 science fiction work, *The Mummy!: Or a Tale of the Twenty-Second Century*, by Jane C. Loudon contains one of the earliest examples of the mummy in literature. Then in 1903, Bram Stoker published the horror novel "*The Jewel of Seven Stars*" containing an archeologist's attempt to revive an ancient mummy.[45]

"In the wake of the 1922 discovery of Tutankhamun's tomb, Mummies found their way onto the silver screen starting with The Mummy a 1932 horror film starring Boris Karloff as a revived ancient Egyptian priest. It was the first of the Mummy horror genre."[46]

VAMPIRES

Count Dracula, the King of the Vampires, from Transylvania. Stories of beings consuming blood or flesh of the living appear in many cultures back to ancient times. Many of the myths of what we know as "vampire behavior" began during the medieval period, but vampires proper originate in folklore.

Vampires were widely reported from Eastern Europe in the late 17th and 18th centuries and appeared in poems and fiction as early as the mid-1700s. *"No effort to depict*

---

45 "Mummy." *Wikipedia: The Free Encyclopedia*. Wikimedia Foundation, Inc. 24 March 2012. Web. 24 March 2012. <http://en.wikipedia.org/wiki/Mummy>

46 "Mummy." *Wikipedia: The Free Encyclopedia*. Wikimedia Foundation, Inc. 24 March 2012. Web. 24 March 2012. <http://en.wikipedia.org/wiki/Mummy>

vampires in popular fiction was as influential or as definitive as ram Stoker's Dracula (1897)." [47]

Of course the name Dracula, conjures up the image of the Count who drinks the blood of his victims. They too become vampires themselves. The only way to kill them is through a stake in their heart. Legends probably started from the acts of bats with their prey--nonhuman prey--usually other, smaller animal species. The bats would come out at night hunt their prey and drink their blood. The remains of the prey were pale, lifeless, bloodless carcasses. So, if you were looking for a tale to scare children, to keep rivals from your property or enhance a reputation of power, here was a great story. The legend has been around for centuries. A legend that captures the imagination can last a very long time.

Scientists tell us the only modern bats that actually drink the blood of wildlife live in the Americas. We don't know if vampire bats were more widespread in centuries past. Perhaps the aggressive nocturnal activity of other bats alone was enough to instilled irrational fear in people. [48]

Other blood sucking creatures and insects may have also given rise to accounts of bloodsucking beings returning from the dead. Some, like Vampire Bats and Vampire (Darwin's) Finches are only (currently) documented in specific habitats. More widespread are insects and parasites known to have been companions in civilization for centuries. There are certainly many examples of creatures who were and are "out

47 "Vampire." *Wikipedia: The Free Encyclopedia.* Wikimedia Foundation, Inc. 24 March 2012. Web. 24 March 2012. <http://en.wikipedia.org/wiki/Vampire>
48 "Hematophagy." *Wikipedia: The Free Encyclopedia.* Wikimedia Foundation, Inc. 24 March 2012. Web. 24 March 2012. <http://en.wikipedia.org/wiki/Hematophagy>

for blood" including mosquitoes, ticks (who can drink up to 600 times their body weight in blood), lampreys that latch on to other fish and sometimes humans to drink their blood, bedbugs that come out at night to drink blood and leave painful bites, Kissing bugs that suck blood from your face leaving large marks and sometimes allergic reactions, fleas, lice and the ever-popular leeches that leave you to bleed even after they're removed.

Many are known to spread disease. Some cause visible or painful symptoms.

Imagine waking to find a bloody wound, blood on your clothing and possibly a swollen face. Or to soon succumb to a disease like Typhus, fevers, malaria, or the plague. It's not much of a leap to imagine some supernatural blood-sucking being has caused the disease.

Of course, if you see a bloated red-faced creature with blood dripping from the mouth or nose and a black cape, you can be pretty sure it's a "Vampire".

The fixation with a being stealing your blood is ancient. The *"notion of vampirism has existed for millennia; cultures such as the Mesopotamians, Hebrews, Ancient Greeks, and Romans"* [49] Almost every nation has some tale of blood-drinking. Similar activities were attributed to demons or spirits who would eat flesh and drink blood; even the Devil was considered synonymous with the vampire at some periods in history.

---

[49] "Vampire Folklore by Region." *Wikipedia: The Free Encyclopedia*. Wikimedia Foundation, Inc. 24 March 2012. Web. 24 March 2012.
<http://en.wikipedia.org/wiki/Vampire_folklore_by_region>

Southeastern European legends of actual "vampires" were documented in the early 18th "when verbal traditions of many ethnic groups of the region were recorded and published." They included a whole range of characterizations including "revenants" (dead entities returning) of evil beings, suicide victims, or witches" [50] Some were caused by possession or the bite of another vampire. "Belief in such legends became so pervasive that in some areas it caused mass hysteria and even public executions of people believed to be vampires." [51]

ZOMBIES

Flesh eating zombies. Really?

What will we do after we pass out of this existence? Once our vessel, the body which housed us is separated from our energy, we don't need to keep the body going. Logically, without a body, we would not desire food or drink.

While the "flesh-eating" part is of more recent origin, the reanimated component has some identifiable sources and even has some plausible explanations (And no, I don't believe we become infected by some biological virus created in a lab on Sci-Fi which will reanimate us.)

The well-documented Zombie beliefs of West Africa and Haiti concern *"animated corpses brought back to life through some*

50 "Vampire." *Wikipedia: The Free Encyclopedia.* Wikimedia Foundation, Inc. 24 March 2012. Web. 24 March 2012 <http://en.wikipedia.org/wiki/Vampire>
51 "Vampire." *Wikipedia: The Free Encyclopedia.* Wikimedia Foundation, Inc. 24 March 2012. Web. 24 March 2012. <http://en.wikipedia.org/wiki/Vampire>

magical or mystical means."[52] and is associated with the practice of Dark magic in Vodou.

A stiffened gait and death-like trance are usually associated with zombies. Victims exist as captives to another in a state of virtual slavery. Very similar myths appear in South Africa. Some aspects of zombies may have been incorporated into fictional works as early as the 19th century. [53]

The figure of the zombie appears in fiction, as early as the 1929 novel, *The Magic Island*. Later, with Bela Lugosi as the evil voodoo master, in the 1932 *White Zombie*, the public's attention was further engaged with zombies. [54] [55]

Zombie fiction is *"now a sizeable sub-genre of horror"* due in large part to George A. Romero's 1968 film The Night of the Living Dead. The film represents a *"new version of the zombie, distinct from that described in Haitian religion"*[56] and probably the first instance of the "flesh-eating" behavior.

Some researchers suspect Vodou in Africa and Haiti may involve the use of drugs (neurotoxins and psychoactive drugs) to produce a death-like state in which the will of the victim would be entirely subject to the bokor or sorcerer. This drug-induced condition could produce a death-like state

52 "Zombie ." *Wikipedia: The Free Encyclopedia*. Wikimedia Foundation, Inc. 24 March 2012. Web. 24 March 2012. <http://en.wikipedia.org/wiki/Zombie>
53 "Undead." *Wikipedia: The Free Encyclopedia*. Wikimedia Foundation, Inc. 24 March 2012. Web. 24 March 2012. <http://en.wikipedia.org/wiki/Undead>
54 "Zombie." *Wikipedia: The Free Encyclopedia*. Wikimedia Foundation, Inc. 24 March 2012. Web. 24 March 2012. <http://en.wikipedia.org/wiki/Zombie>
55 "White Zombie (film)." *Wikipedia: The Free Encyclopedia*. Wikimedia Foundation, Inc. 24 March 2012. Web. 24 March 2012. <http://en.wikipedia.org/wiki/White_Zombie_%28film%29>
56 "Zombie." *Wikipedia: The Free Encyclopedia*. Wikimedia Foundation, Inc. 24 March 2012. Web. 24 March 2012. <http://en.wikipedia.org/wiki/Zombie>

leading to a burial. Such conditions could be mistaken for the reanimation of a corpse from the grave. [57]

Another disorder implicated for zombie behavior is Catalepsy. Symptoms include a rigid body, (like the rigid limbs of a zombie) and a slowing down of bodily functions like breathing sometimes to the point of temporary unconsciousness. [58]

Belief in the vampire, an animated corpse that remains in its grave by day and emerges to prey on the living at night, has sometimes been attributed to premature burial. [59]

It is interesting to note the widespread fear of live burial in Western culture during the nineteenth century. The fear was so great that coffins were sometimes equipped with special emergency devices to allow the "corpse" to call for help should he or she turn out to be still living. From the 1840s through the early 20th century there were more than a dozen patented devices for detecting life in buried persons. [60] Victorians even organized a *Society for the Prevention of People Being Buried Alive*. Edgar Allen Poe took advantage of

57 "Zombie" *Wikipedia: The Free Encyclopedia*. Wikimedia Foundation, Inc. 24 March 2012. Web. 24 March 2012. <http://en.wikipedia.org/wiki/Zombie>
58 "Catalepsy." *Wikipedia: The Free Encyclopedia*. Wikimedia Foundation, Inc. 24 March 2012. Web. 24 March 2012.< http://en.wikipedia.org/wiki/Catalepsy>
59 "Premature Burial." *Wikipedia: The Free Encyclopedia*. Wikimedia Foundation, Inc. 24 March 2012. Web. 24 March 2012. <http://en.wikipedia.org/wiki/The_Premature_Burial>
60 Richard Van Vleck, "Signals from the Grave", *American Artifacts*, Issue 45. July 1999, Web. 24 March 2012. <http://www.americanartifacts.com/smma/life/life.htm> with permission

the public's absorption with the topic with "*The Premature Burial*", a horror short story on the theme. (1844). [61]

And there were indeed accounts of people being buried alive. Sometimes the truth can be more terrifying than fiction.

Similar symptoms have been described in hypnotism and self-induced trances. Such trances played on another primal fear– the same fear of being buried alive.

"*In cases of trance the physical body assumes an appearance resembling death, and in many cases not to be distinguished from it in appearance merely. In this state persons have frequently been supposed to be dead, and have been buried alive, even while they were conscious of what was going on...* "[62]

GHOSTS

Ghosts are **not** myths. And although I do not like to use the term "Ghosts" myself, it has been used in different cultures to describe the form we take on in the next life.

References to "ghosts" or "spirits" are virtually universal around the world and throughout time. Belief in the enduring spirit of a deity or loved one is a "cultural universal"

---

61 "Premature Burial." *Wikipedia: The Free Encyclopedia*. Wikimedia Foundation, Inc. 24 March 2012. Web. 24 March 2012. <http://en.wikipedia.org/wiki/The_Premature_Burial>
62 Joel Tiffany, "Lectures on spiritualism, being a series of lectures on the phenomena...(1851)", *Internet Archive: American Libraries*. 24 March 2012 <http://archive.org/details/lecturesonspirio1tiffgoog>

and probably predates any documented mythological or religious reference. [63]

We find very early references to spirits or ghosts around the world. The earliest are in the form of legends or myths.

In the middle-near east, the cradle of civilization, we find Babylonian references at least as early as the 7th century BC, with Sumerian "Gidim". Suggestions of ghosts are found in other early Mesopotamian states as early as the 3rd century BC, with Greek mentions at least as early as the 8th century BC in Homer and Roman references at least as early as 50BC. Egyptian indication of ghosts is probably well before the Book of the Dead at around 1550 BC and in the Chinese culture at least as early as 800 BC. They are found within Japanese culture probably at least as early as 700 AD and in Tibet perhaps as early as 650 BC. Other early allusions to ghosts exist in Malay, Polynesian, Philippine, Indonesian, African and Asian Indian cultures.

There are indications of ghosts for the Maya before 1550, for the Aztecs as early as the 13th century and in the Norse religion at least as early as the 13th century.

One of the very earliest documented myths containing a reference to ghosts is the Epic of Gilgamesh from Mesopotamia. (The most complete version existing today is preserved from a 7th-century BC library collection.) [64]

---

63 "Ghost." *Wikipedia: The Free Encyclopedia*. Wikimedia Foundation, Inc. 24 March 2012. Web. 24 March 2012. < http://en.wikipedia.org/wiki/Ghost>
64 "Epic of Gilgamesh." *Wikipedia: The Free Encyclopedia*. Wikimedia Foundation, Inc. 24 March 2012. Web. 24 March 2012. <http://en.wikipedia.org/wiki/Epic_of_Gilgamesh>

"Part of the story relates Endiku's death, the adventures of his ghost in the underworld, and the eventual return back to the world." There is even reason to believe that the Old Testament's flood refers to the same flood described in the Babylonian epic of Gilgamesh. [65]

"Belief in ghosts in European folklore is characterized by the recurring fear of "returning" or revenant deceased who may harm the living." [66]

Up until the 18th century *"Belief in the soul and an afterlife remained near universal."* [67]

Spirits, however (or ghosts if you prefer), do not fly around in a white sheet and look like Casper the Friendly Ghost. They do not say "boo" or hang out in cemeteries. The term apparition is used in the paranormal community to describe the form by which we present ourselves; our energy form. They may be perceived as a solid form or as a fleeting movement. Some people also refer to them as shadow people due to the fact that they often appear as dark silhouettes.

"Ghosts" can manifest as a partial form as a whole figure. Most people will never see a true apparition. Even the special equipment used by paranormal groups such as night

---

65 "Epic of Gilgamesh." *Wikipedia: The Free Encyclopedia*. Wikimedia Foundation, Inc. 24 March 2012. Web. 24 March 2012. <http://en.wikipedia.org/wiki/Epic_of_Gilgamesh>
66 "Ghost." *Wikipedia: The Free Encyclopedia*. Wikimedia Foundation, Inc. 24 March 2012. Web. 24 March 2012. <http://en.wikipedia.org/wiki/Ghost>
67 "Ghost." *Wikipedia: The Free Encyclopedia*. Wikimedia Foundation, Inc. 24 March 2012. Web. 24 March 2012. <http://en.wikipedia.org/wiki/Ghost>

vision cameras and full-spectrum cameras cannot guarantee a visual confirmation. The spirit or ghost uses their energy and the energy of the environment to attempt to transform themselves into a figure. We will discuss more about the manifestation of spirits and operations in a future chapter.

POLTERGEISTS (ONE CATEGORY OF GHOST)

As I've suggested earlier, I have never experienced a Poltergeist as most people imagine them–destructive, trouble-making spirits who haunt a person or place. Fictional poltergeists are supposed to throw or move inanimate objects, make noises like knocking, pounding or banging or even engage in physical attacks. Recorded cases date back to the 1st century and references appear in many cultures and countries. [68]

I have researched and witnessed events intended to capture the attention of a living person that can include sounds and moving items. However, I suspect many reports that go beyond this behavior--harmful or destructive events--are faked, embellished or were due to explainable causes. Poltergeist activity might be attributed to minor geologic activity, heating systems and pipes, rats, shutters or unusual building acoustics.

The example of Borley Rectory in England suggests how a human attempt to draw attention away from a wife's illicit affair with a roomer might develop into a more troublesome

68 "Poltergeist." *Wikipedia: The Free Encyclopedia.* Wikimedia Foundation, Inc. 24 March 2012. Web. 24 March 2012. <http://en.wikipedia.org/wiki/Poltergeist>

"Poltergeist". Want to fool around? Blame those noises on the poltergeist. [69]

Borley Rectory was a Victorian era mansion located in the village of Borley, Essex, England that at one point acquired the description of "The Most Haunted House in England" [70] It was widely covered in the press.

"Between the 1920s and late 1935, reported incidents, included bell-ringing, windows shattering, stones, bottle-throwing and wall-writing, and a daughter locked in a room with no key"[71]. The wife reported a whole range of poltergeist phenomena including being thrown from her bed. The wife later admitted that she was having a sexual relationship with the lodger, and that she used 'paranormal' explanations to cover up her liaisons. Despite the hoax, later investigators speculated some **non-violent** paranormal activity in the location.

Once again, this myth of aggressive poltergeists was likely created from stories passed around from tribe to tribe long before TV or movies. Because people since the dawn of time have not truly understood what happens to us when we pass, stories had to be made up. Most are not based on any facts or research, just conjecture. This is how most myths came to be. And this is just one more. Makes for good TV for some, but for me, I find it insulting.

---

69 "Borley Rectory." *Wikipedia: The Free Encyclopedia.* Wikimedia Foundation, Inc. 24 March 2012. Web. 24 March 2012. <http://en.wikipedia.org/wiki/Borley_Rectory>
70 "Borley Rectory." *Wikipedia: The Free Encyclopedia.* Wikimedia Foundation, Inc. 24 March 2012. Web. 24 March 2012. <http://en.wikipedia.org/wiki/Borley_Rectory>
71 "Borley Rectory." *Wikipedia: The Free Encyclopedia.* Wikimedia Foundation, Inc. 24 March 2012. Web. 24 March 2012. <http://en.wikipedia.org/wiki/Borley_Rectory>

While my personal experience with "poltergeists" is limited, I can say that in every case, there was turmoil in the home or around the people in question. Claims of activity seemed to center around a particular person under duress and were accompanied by an extremely high negativity surrounding that individual.

One case involved a 16 year old girl. Distress at the separation of her parents was coupled with alienation from her peers at school. The overall stressful nature of a teen life magnified the girl's inability to coop with the emotional stressors all around her. She began wetting the bed and urinating on herself in school. Her dreams became nightmares with repeated visions of her body being taken over by a "gruesome, cold entity". Her body soon became covered with a rash. She felt she was being pursued by an evil entity and the teen began hearing voices telling her to hurt herself and her family. Next, items in her room would be found thrown or broken. The words "Hate" and "Die" were scribbled on her bedroom wall.

Fearing her daughter was being harmed by a demon, her mother asked for help from a paranormal group (I am happy to say this was not any group with whom I have ever been associated.). After the investigation, the group determined her daughter was "haunted" and possessed by a "demon" or "Poltergeist". "She needed a cleansing"... What she really needed was plain old help.

I was directed to this family by a co-worker. The magnitude of anxiety and stress surrounding this young girl was immediately evident in our conversations. The negativity that she carried with her had overtaken her ability to accurately perceive what was truly happening. She was not "possessed"; she was however, manifesting unusual, subconscious behaviors due to the increase of her negative energy.

My recommendation was to seek counseling. With professional help she was able to come to terms with the changes around her. I am happy to say, she was able to put these issues behind her. She learned how to develop her coping abilities. The activities have stopped.

This instance, as with most claims, could be debunked as the result of common occurrences that were misunderstood or misidentified by one or more individuals.

Unfortunately, as with other cases in this book, falsehoods, misconceptions and a little bit of hysteria created a pseudo-paranormal situation. An undereducated paranormal group contributed to an unnecessarily traumatic incident for this very young, very vulnerable, girl.

The matter of poltergeists is surrounded by skepticism and sensationalism for good reason. Scientific study of the frequency and legitimacy of poltergeist activity has been conducted over several decades. Many reports were found to be frauds or the result of explainable circumstances. Most researchers have concluded that the majority of **legitimate** manifestations are NOT the result of possessions, or occult practices, but simply of the body and mind's reaction to extreme stress. Some theorize that this activity can also be attributed to "Psychokinesis." [72] [73]

So, let us suppose, as I do, that some, but not all, spirit activity is authentic. The question of the compatibility of spirit contact and religion remains an important topic for many people. Some who study the scriptures interpret biblical passages to state that ghosts do not exist and/or all spirits are of evil origin. Further, they believe that all communication with the dead is forbidden by God.

Others scholars do not find ghosts inconsistent with the Bible. They also differentiate between communication and deliberate attempts at divination and foretelling the future.

There are several biblical references that are often cited to support whether, according to the Old and New Testaments, ghosts can exist; whether humans can communicate with them and what contact is forbidden by God and why:

2 Corinthians 5:1, 6-8 and 1 Corinthians 15:51,
Matthew 14:25-27, Matthew 8:28-34 and Matthew 10:1-4,

1 Samuel chapter 28:7-25 and 11-
1 Thessalonians 4:13

The prohibition of what is commonly translated as *"communication with the dead"* probably refers to Necromancy, which involves more than just communication with the dead.

---

72 "Enfield Poltergeist." *Wikipedia: The Free Encyclopedia.* Wikimedia Foundation, Inc. 24 March 2012. Web. 24 March 2012. <http://en.wikipedia.org/wiki/Enfield_Poltergeist>
73 "Psychokinesis." *Wikipedia: The Free Encyclopedia.* Wikimedia Foundation, Inc. 24 March 2012. Web. 24 March 2012. <http://en.wikipedia.org/wiki/Psychokinesis>

Necromancy was a common pagan practice before and during early Christian eras, so I believe it is worth exploring the definition of necromancy. *"Necromancy is a claimed form of magic involving communication with the deceased–**either by summoning their spirit as an apparition** or **raising them bodily–for the purpose of divination, imparting the means to foretell future events** or **discover hidden knowledge.** "The term may sometimes be used in a more general sense to refer to black magic or witchcraft."* [74]

Some references even suggest a deliberate strategy behind certain prohibitions.

With regard to witchcraft in Judaism, Maimonides "claimed that the Biblical prohibitions regarding it were precisely to wean the Israelites from practices related to idolatry [...] while others acknowledge that magic exists, but is forbidden on the basis that it usually involves the worship of other gods." [75]

I am certainly no theologian or expert on religion. I can only share my own personal experiences. After combining that study with all the spirits I actually experience, I have come to believe that the spirits **normally** around us are good and helpful entities. They are **not** sent by evil forces. I don't know if they are sent by God, whether they are "guardian angels" or if they appear through the assistance of angels, but sometimes they **behave** as personal guardians to us.

---

74 "Necromancy." *Wikipedia: The Free Encyclopedia.* Wikimedia Foundation, Inc. 24 March 2012. Web. 24 March 2012. http://en.wikipedia.org/wiki/Necromancy
75 "Witchcraft." *Wikipedia: The Free Encyclopedia.* Wikimedia Foundation, Inc. 24 March 2012. Web. 24 March 2012. <http://en.wikipedia.org/wiki/Witchcraft>

Altogether we can see the influence of primal fears, masterful storytellers and earthly political considerations in our 21st century view of myths. We can also attribute attempts at translating concepts that have no true equivalent, a lack of knowledge about chemical and biological toxins and perhaps the all-too-human desire to find a scapegoat. The targets of attempts to blame were often someone who was different–poor, a non-churchgoer, a quarrelsome neighbor, or a gifted or successful individual. As you approach reports of any sort of paranormal activity, keep these influences in mind.

Chapter 5 What Makes Us Believe ?

This chapter is to review some of the cultural differences and belief systems regarding the afterlife which are found from one group to another. Most cultures have some belief in life after death or the afterlife. However, the details--when it begins, how it occurs and any personal transformations, differ from culture to culture.

For atheists, there is no recognition of life after death. You are here and then you cease to exist.

Experiments have shown our earliest infant cognition does not include a "continuity of being". If a baby can't see you, even if you are merely behind a screen, you do not exist. If a baby cannot touch you, then you are not real in their world. An infant will be puzzled or surprised if you appear once again.

I believe it is human nature to seek explanations for what occurs around us.

Atheists believe what is rationally explainable. There is no expectation of either an ascension into a heaven or a descent into hell. Life is "the now" and any speculation of what occurs afterward is not worth discussing. If it can't be physically explored; if it can't be fully explained, it can't be real.

Realistically, this is a good philosophy. A protection from endless worry about your behavior here on earth or the care and good deeds you bestow upon others. It doesn't matter.

So how would you go about proving a continuation of existence after death to someone who feels this way? Well, you can't.

Just as respect for others' values is important in daily living, it's important for a medium to be sensitive to clients' beliefs. I have given readings to many atheists or proclaimed atheists. They would report that I was 100% accurate in my reading; they were even impressed by my ability. Yet, the same individuals claim contact did not alter their beliefs on life after death. They can't "see or touch" that energy, or can they?

We don't know because they won't try. They go beyond skepticism. They **refuse** to believe.

I remember one reading for a young girl who professed to being an atheist for 10 years. She was only coming to me for information to write a paper for school. During the reading she sat quietly taking notes. Her mother's spirit (who arrived with the girl) told me repeatedly "*She doesn't believe because of me, I never believed either.*" When I told this to the young girl, she looked at me with a blush and a facial expression I will never forget--part anger, part sadness. She stated one thing, "*You are a liar*".

I was not a liar, but her mother desperately needed the girl to hear her, to feel her. I asked mom to give me one thing, very personal, about her daughter, hoping it would help us go forward. She stated she was sorry she yelled at her daughter when the jewelry box fell and broke. The young girl looked at me and stated "*It was the first time I ever heard my mother yell.*" Her mother stated "*Tell her she's my pumpkin.*" She began to cry. I felt we had made a break, but I was wrong. The conversation continued; she returned to taking notes. I asked her if she would like to feel her mom's touch. She stated "*Why? She's not here.*" I thought to myself "*How can you say that? Are you really going to pretend that you don't believe? Are you going to do this to yourself? To your mother? Is denying belief more important??*" I was perplexed and saddened. What a missed opportunity. She finished her notes; thanked me and left. I stood there wondering if there was something else I could have or should have done.

I really suspect the skepticism of atheists is a deep-seated mindset, not really a belief system. It comes from something deep down inside them; maybe an event, a bad childhood, something so difficult they refuse to believe even when the truth is staring them right in the face.

I often think of that young girl and her beautiful mother who so wanted her daughter to believe. I also wonder about the school paper. *How did she write it? Did the writing process change her mind at all? Was her paper written with less skepticism than it would have been before our session? And if not, did her paper help to influence others to deny or ridicule spirits? Is that how it starts? Can articles or books have the power to dissuade or convince us? Will mine?* I guess I'll never know.

As I said before there is nothing wrong with being skeptical and I encourage you to question things that don't seem right or make sense. That's just smart. But there **is** something very wrong with blocking out any opportunity for learning.

Another belief is based upon the law of conservation of energy which I addressed earlier. If energy cannot be created or destroyed, but only transformed, then where were we or where was our energy before we were us? Were we somewhere in the universe waiting to be born? Or is this a rationale for the theory of reincarnation?

The theory of **Reincarnation** has been around for thousands of years. The New World Encyclopedia defines the word reincarnation from Latin to mean *"to be made flesh again"*. Some cultures believe that everyone has lived many lives reincarnating into the same family. Others feel that you take on a whole different animate life; while still others believe you can reincarnate into an inanimate object such as a chair or a piece of jewelry.

People who believe they have been reincarnated often state they are plagued by dreams and memories they cannot possibly have had or explain. There are even cases studies of individuals and young children who knew their names, shared skills and interests, recognized homes or the circumstances of their deaths with incredible accuracy. In some cases a physical resemblance to the past-life person is noted. Even more incredibly, birthmarks or abnormalities are found in the same places on the body. [76]

Having the same ailment may be coincidence, but it is hard to account for recognition of specific people and places--and other undocumented details. If you imagine the situation of those with recurring dreams and memories, it is easy to appreciate their need to explore the subject in hopes of getting some answers for themselves.

The idea of your energy just floating around in the universe waiting for you to "be" sounds a little silly. So perhaps the

---

76 "Reincarnation Research." *Wikipedia: The Free Encyclopedia.* Wikimedia Foundation, Inc. 24 March 2012. Web. 24 March 2012. <http://en.wikipedia.org/wiki/Reincarnation_research>

regeneration or change of our energy from one person to another is credible.

I find disbelievers will tell you that the brain is highly suggestible and retains information that we don't realize we have absorbed. To some degree, this is true. Our brains are capable of storing vast amounts of data from all our senses involuntarily. It is plausible that our mind could recreate something we have seen before. However, it is **not** credible to imagine we inadvertently acquire such **specific** information about particular people and places. I remain open to the notion.

Some reincarnation theories and cultures like that of the **Inuit Indians** view the process of reincarnation as a rite of passage. They feel each cycle of life allows you to give and gain knowledge that is carried to the next. Further, they believe this knowledge helps you to become a better person enriching both your life **and** that of the community. They strive to make each life the best. The emphasis is not on philosophy, but on the benefit to their culture.

Other traditions have a firm belief in an afterlife, but not in reincarnation.

The **Celts**, share a belief in life after death as another, separate world, but one which could interact with the living. They believe people within the mortal world could stumble into the other world and return to find that they been gone for years. To speed the transition of the dead, windows are opened for the souls to have a clear path. It is then the soul is separated from whatever earthly physical manifestations the body had prior to death.

Some civilizations require meticulous preparation for the afterlife. The **Mayans**, a culture strongly influenced by religion, led lives in fear of the destructive nature of their gods. They held a reverence for death. Death was a journey with the possibility of rebirth. Great care was taken to prepare them for the next life. Maize was placed in the mouth--a symbol of rebirth. A stone or bead for currency for the journey and other offerings were also provided. The graves always face North and West in the direction of the heavens. They believed the two worlds of life and after-life were cyclical; the physical world was unavoidably tied to the supernatural world in repeating cycle with no beginning or end. [77] [78] [79]

Conceptions of the after-life are not universally pleasant. Another group called the **Sumerians** felt that there was no wonderful, restful afterlife, only pain and suffering. [80] They believed that all men were inherently evil and are never able to obtain any sort of paradise. [81] Paradise was reserved for the Gods. Their afterworld, a place between the great above and the great below, was governed by strict laws just as their earthly lives had been. Even in death they could not escape

---

77 "Hell." *Wikipedia: The Free Encyclopedia*. Wikimedia Foundation, Inc. 24 March 2012. Web. 24 March 2012. <http://en.wikipedia.org/wiki/Hell>

78 "Maya_religion." *Wikipedia: The Free Encyclopedia*. Wikimedia Foundation, Inc. 24 March 2012. Web. 24 March 2012. <http://en.wikipedia.org/wiki/Maya_religion>

79 "Maya Religion: Afterlife: Underworld and Paradise." *Wikipedia: The Free Encyclopedia*. Wikimedia Foundation, Inc. 24 March 2012. Web. 24 March 2012. http://en.wikipedia.org/wiki/Maya_religion#Afterlife:_underworld_and_ paradise>

80 "Sumer." *Wikipedia: The Free Encyclopedia*. Wikimedia Foundation, Inc. 24 March 2012. Web. 24 March 2012. <http://en.wikipedia.org/wiki/Sumer>

81 "Sumer:Religion." *Wikipedia: The Free Encyclopedia*. Wikimedia Foundation, Inc. 24 March 2012. Web. 24 March 2012. <http://en.wikipedia.org/wiki/Sumer#Religion>

the rules. There was no divine compassion, only a grim underworld of dust and clay from which there was no release. We may have more to learn of their practices as more archaeological evidence emerges. Some scholars suggest we may find the idea of suffering was a purification for a return to life.

Another culture, that of ancient **Egyptians,** had a complex set of beliefs about death that evolved over the centuries. Through much of their ancient history, they believed death was a stepping stone to a new kind of existence. Initially it was only royalty that lived on, in later eras, the *"possibility of a paradisiacal afterlife extended to everyone."* [82] They believed a human soul has the Ba and The Akh. The Akh went to heaven and the Ba remained on earth. And, since the Ba remained with the body of the deceased, it needed to be embalmed for preservation. [83] Other *"funeral rituals were intended to release the Ba from the body so that it could move freely, and to rejoin it with the Ka so that it could live on as an Akh."* [84]

During some periods the concept of the Akh developed into a sort of roaming dead being that could do either harm or good to persons still living. In the world of the living, it could help family members but also inflict punishments through

---

82 "Ancient Egyptian Religion." *Wikipedia: The Free Encyclopedia.* Wikimedia Foundation, Inc. 24 March 2012. Web. 24 March 2012.
<http://en.wikipedia.org/wiki/Ancient_Egyptian_religion>
83 "Ancient Egyptian Religion." *Wikipedia: The Free Encyclopedia.* Wikimedia Foundation, Inc. 24 March 2012. Web. 24 March 2012.
<http://en.wikipedia.org/wiki/Ancient_Egyptian_religion>
84 "Ancient Egyptian Religion." *Wikipedia: The Free Encyclopedia.* Wikimedia Foundation, Inc. 24 March 2012. Web. 24 March 2012.
<http://en.wikipedia.org/wiki/Ancient_Egyptian_religion>

interactions with other entities and deities and *"to some degree magically affect events there".* [85][86]

The **Aztec** Indians strongly believed in an afterlife. Their beliefs were quite involved since they had adopted concepts from previous Mesoamerican civilizations. These included a model of multiple levels of heavens and hells.

However, it was the way the Aztecs died rather than the way they lived that determined where they would go. Their "after place" was very complex, multi-leveled and multi-segmented. Fallen warriors and women who died in childbirth went directly to the sun god. Those who died from less glorious causes found a dark and dismal underworld. Only after a long, treacherous journey filled with challenges would one reach Mictlan, presumably a better place than the other levels. There was even a special place for those drowned or had otherwise been killed by manifestations of water, Tlalocan. [87]

Their assumptions were based on a great, on-going sacrifice (sometimes self-sacrifice) to perpetuate the Universe. Their views gave sacrifice (including human sacrifice) an honored

---

85 "Egyptian Soul:Akh." *Wikipedia: The Free Encyclopedia.* Wikimedia Foundation, Inc. 24 March 2012. Web. 24 March 2012. <http://en.wikipedia.org/wiki/Egyptian_soul#Akh>
86 "Ancient Egyptian Religion." *Wikipedia: The Free Encyclopedia.* Wikimedia Foundation, Inc. 24 March 2012. Web. 24 March 2012.
<http://en.wikipedia.org/wiki/Ancient_Egyptian_religion>
87 "Aztec Religion:Cosmology and Ritual." *Wikipedia: The Free Encyclopedia.* Wikimedia Foundation, Inc. 24 March 2012. Web. 24 March 2012.
<http://en.wikipedia.org/wiki/Aztec_religion#Cosmology_and_ritual>

role. Both Gods and humans had a responsibility in sacrifice. [88]

One observation found in varied cultures is an All Souls Day or Day of the Dead. In Mexico, it is a national holiday to honor family and friends who have died. Families hope to encourage visits by the souls so the deceased can hear the prayers of the living. Many such festivals are held in November as the days grow shorter and fall transitions to the "death" of winter–perhaps symbolic of death as a transition from one life to another. [89]

As you can see, many different cultures have some belief system regarding where we go after this life. The sources and practices may be different from ours, but they are based on one fact. There is a universal need to know what happens to us when we leave this life.

Across the board, we long to know that we will see and be with our loved ones again. My belief system includes components of many of the ones we've just discussed. However, I believe the way of the Hopi Indians comes closest to my personal beliefs.

When we look at the Hopi Indians, it is interesting to note the similarities of their beliefs about an afterlife to those of the Northeastern Tribes such as the Penobscot, Abnaki and Passamaquoddy.

---

88 "Aztec Religion:Cosmology and Ritual." *Wikipedia: The Free Encyclopedia.* Wikimedia Foundation, Inc. 24 March 2012. Web. 24 March 2012.
<http://en.wikipedia.org/wiki/Aztec_religion#Cosmology_and_ritual>
89 "Day of the Dead." *Wikipedia: The Free Encyclopedia.* Wikimedia Foundation, Inc. 24 March 2012. Web. 24 March 2012. <http://en.wikipedia.org/wiki/Day_of_the_Dead>

I was fortunate to gain some understanding of Northeastern beliefs from my personal relationships with tribe members. A cornerstone of their belief is the separation of the soul from the body. It differs from traditional western religious beliefs since "the soul" does not depart this world, nor does it remain in the here and now. "The breath" leaves the body upon death andmoves to another sphere. It becomes a part of another plane of existence, not worse or better than this one. From this side-by-side plane, the "soul" can interact with our plane to provide continuing assistance in the daily lives of family and friends.

Similarly, the Hopi believe in a breath, or "Spirit of the Breath", that becomes a part of another realm and can mingle with nature and come back to their people. It still interacts with our world, just in another plane. [90]

Continuation of life–living, seeing, smelling, feeling is the foundation of this belief. The breath is what the Hopi refer to as the soul which is said to live forever after the body dies. This belief is more in line with what I see and have seen-- what I know to be true.

It always amazes me that, regardless of where you go, whatever your culture or belief system may be, you can usually find a link to a belief system cemented in the afterlife.

The preparation for transition from this life into the next seems to be universal. The thought of living a good life and thoughts of earning a peaceful afterlife are the goals of most. Some would say these concepts were perpetuated to

---

90 "Fred_Kaboti." *Wikipedia: The Free Encyclopedia.* Wikimedia Foundation, Inc. 2 May 2012. Web. 2 May 2012. <http://en.wikipedia.org/wiki/Fred_Kabotie>

ensure individuals in a culture behave in a customary way. Treat others with kindness or risk a final end, an eternity of torture or whatever seems most terrible in that culture.

I am not saying that there is no basis of fact in what I like to call "the scaring of men" philosophy. Being raised in the Catholic Church, I saw enough fear being placed in parishioner's heads. The fear of retaliation by a vengeful God is promised if you are not a good citizen, neighbor or family member. However, for the wide range of cultures since the beginning of time to have come to the same conclusion is worthy of note. I, for one, do not believe this is coincidental. That so many cultures set down, sometimes elaborate, steps as the necessary preparation to ensure a peaceful and fulfilling afterlife is remarkable.

We prepare many times throughout our life for changes in our normal lifestyle. We prepare for our wedding; prepare for a new baby; we prepare for retirement. Why in our culture do we not do a better job of preparing for the next life? Sure there are life insurance plans, and advanced directives, but I'm talking about the actual preparation of our selves, our families and our souls to begin the next journey.

As much as we prepare for this inevitable time, it is equally important for our loved ones to prepare themselves. How does one prepare for a life without their loved one **physically** beside them? I tell people I think the best gift I can offer is to help them understand what will happen next; what to do and what not to do once their loved one has passed.

I help prepare family members and loved ones who remain **here** for a new life and new type of relationship, not the end of one. There is nothing morbid; there is nothing wrong with preparing ourselves for the next step of our life. People who prepare for anything have less stress, are better organized and in some ways have a better understanding and acceptance of the next journey that awaits them.

Chapter 6   A Society of Believers...
An Informal Survey

When contemplating the type of information I wanted to put in my book, I felt the need to include information that analyzed how others feel about the afterlife. What do they believe? So I set to the task of collecting data from as many different people as I could. This information was collected locally, so opinions may vary from region to region and country to country. I wanted to see, in my small universe, how far apart or how close we are in our beliefs and feelings regarding the afterlife.

My questions were simple. They were meant to allow not just simple answers, but for commentary. The first question they were asked: *"Do you believe in an afterlife?"* and *"If so, why and on what do you base these beliefs?"* (i.e. personal variances, religion, society and others). They were also asked to explain if these beliefs were based on any experiences, and, if it was a personal experience, to describe the type of experience.

They were asked their age, sex, ethnicity, educational level and socioeconomic background. When describing their educational level, they were simply asked if they had any college education and, if they had, what was the highest level of completion. For their socio-economic background, they were asked if they consider themselves working, middle or upper middle class. For income level, they were asked to check the box next to what best represented their gross income. This level ranged from $12,000 to $70,000 per year, from $70,000 and $150,000 per year, and from $150,000 to over $200,000 per year.

When discussing their age, they were asked to place a check mark next to the box that best represented their age sample: 18–35, 36–45, 46–65, 66–85 and over 85.

Other items in the sample were: their religion, whether married, single, divorced or widowed, if they were in a domestic partnership, or if they considered themselves bisexual, homosexual or heterosexual.

Approximately 500 of these questionnaires were distributed. I received 466 back. Not bad. The information I collected was astonishing. It was not what I anticipated. However, I will say, I was pleased by the responses.

My biggest surprise was the response to the first question. I had not expected that **all** of the 466 participants would say they believe in an afterlife. I was amazed. I was sure I'd find a small percentage of those who identify themselves as non-believers.

When asked the basis of their belief, it was pretty evenly split between religion and personal experience. Some checked both. The teaching of religion has always played a large role in a person's belief system. However, the belief appears stronger when there is a correlation to a personal experience.

I was also surprised with how freely people expressed their emotions and their "comfort level" with this experience.

It was also remarkable to me that for those who had checked personal experiences, alone or in combination with religion, by far the most were women--by 79%.

I learn a lot about the beliefs of others by talking with people. Women are generally the ones telling me they feel "a sense" about things. They are more likely to acknowledge and describe their experiences. The "sense" for women is especially powerful for scenarios involving their children.

Men, for the most part, do not express the same awareness. I continue to gather material on this topic. Why is this? Is it biological? Do women have a keener sense for these things? Or is it a social phenomenon?

As a cultural norm in many societies, men represent the rational ones, the strong ones; the ones for whom everything is black or white. Do they unintentionally block any unfamiliar events, and disregard their occurrence? In the face of any out-of-the-ordinary event, do they simply tell themselves "nothing happened"?

So, let's say women are too emotional or too highly suggestive and believe everything they see. Who knows which is true; it could be a combination of biological and social behavior.

I do have to say I find it curious that when males tell of unexplainable events, generally speaking, they have already discovered a rational explanation. Despite the "rationalizing" of the scenario, it seems they feel a need to tell me about it "quietly". As a medium, my experience bears out the opinion of the 79%. Women do appear to be more open or comfortable with any experiences they may have.

Age plays its own unique role. The participants of this study ranged in age from 18 to 98. As I said before, I divided the ages into five groups.

The most noticeable differences were at the ends of the scale. The people who acknowledge personal experiences tend to occur in either their young years, (early 20s to mid 30s) or past middle age, (from age 60 up). I tried to come to some type of rationale for the age effect. My only theory, and this is only a theory, is that the years between the mid-30s to 60s are a very busy time for most. Raising children, running a home, working, establishing relationships, providing care to their own parents and helping to raise grandchildren. It may be we have too much going on day-to-day and are preoccupied with "everyday life" at this stage in our lives. Perhaps we simply do not pay attention. Again, this is simply a guess. Since this is only a regional study, disparities by age may not be the same in other regions of the world.

When it came to religion, I was not surprised to find that all the people who classify themselves with any specific religious group believed in **some** form of an afterlife. Most religions have a belief system based upon the continuation of ourselves past our physical life.

The differences dealt with the **type of afterlife** they felt would occur and **when** the afterlife began. The largest segment, Catholic Christians (approximately 65%), believed there is a judging time to take place after death--a time to decide where and with whom you will spend eternity.

Those who identified themselves with the Jewish and Muslim religion (approximately 30%) believe that the entrance into the afterlife is immediate, as is the judgment of what type of afterlife is ahead.

A few other groups who consider themselves spiritual, yet not related to any particular religious group (5%), felt that there is a longer period of atonement. That is to say they feel we stay in a state of limbo until we have righted our wrongs. It is only then that we are allowed to share more life with our loved ones.

So even though responders differed in what type of afterlife we will have, they all agree that death represents not the end, but a change for our spiritual selves.

I did notice a difference in how and why different social economic groups and classes deal with their day-to-day activities in relation to their feelings on the afterlife.

Participants identifying themselves as upper middle to upper class (based upon location, status and income indicated as between 70,000 to over 200,000 per year), stated they agreed with the theory of an afterlife, but were unsure how their actions in this life would affect the quality of their afterlife.

On the other hand, the participants who identify themselves as middle to lower class (based upon location, status and income indicated as between 12,000 to 70,000 per year), believed that they would be rewarded for the good deeds that they did while here. This segment was more likely to draw a direct connection between their actions in this life and the character of their life in the next realm. As one participant stated, *"How kind I am to my family, my neighbors, my friends and myself will be reflected in my happiness and contentment in the afterlife"*.

Why the difference? Some sociologists might suggest that those who experience daily struggle and less favorable conditions need a reason to hope and this hope for something better drives their beliefs. Where those who have more, in a material sense, may tend to worry less about what they need to do to achieve a harmonious afterlife. Perhaps they feel their contributions to less fortunate individuals will guarantee them the type of afterlife they seek.

Again this is open to opinion. I believe it is a combination of all of these beliefs that guide our feelings regarding what, if anything, we to need to do to achieve the extension of this life into another.

Participants who identified themselves as parents felt it was important to teach their children about angels, as guides who protect them. They stated this was important for them as well as their children. It gave them peace of mind to believe that someone was protecting their children from harm. Most of these parents couldn't truly identify with any certainty who or what they thought these angels were. They just "knew" that there was a guiding force surrounding and protecting them and their children from harm.

I found no significant differences between those who were single and those who identified themselves as being married with regard to their belief systems on the afterlife.

The small percentage of participants (.5%), who would identify themselves as transgender or homosexual reported they had a very strong belief in the existence of life after this one. Their responses on all the topics were identical to those in a traditional marriage.

Collecting this data was a daunting task, but I feel it gave me a better appreciation for the thoughts and beliefs of our community and neighbors. With all the many differences we have as a society, all the little idiosyncrasies that make us unique, such as types of food we eat, the clothes we wear, the different lifestyles we lead; we all find comfort in knowing that there is more. This (life) is not "it". We have another opportunity, a whole other life waiting for us. How comforting is that?

When it comes to the overall belief in the afterlife, we all have the same need, desire and wish to know that we will go on. We will continue to live, continue to have more opportunities to share in the lives of our loved ones.

I am very grateful to all those who participated in this research. My inquiries touched on what can be very personal subjects. I appreciate both the time and openness of the responders. My decision to write this book was with the hope of educating and helping others learn how to keep an open mind. What I learned from this process is that, at least on this topic, we really aren't very different from one another.

Thanks again.

Chapter 7 I Want to Believe... Why We Believe

Why we believe is just as important as what we believe. It's equally important to examine why some choose **not** to believe.

I think it is easier to explain what makes people accept the idea of life after death. I don't think it is as straightforward to understand why people don't.

So we will start here.

I have met many people in my life who say *"I don't believe because I just don't."*, that's illogical. If people stated *"I don't believe because I have never sensed or felt or heard anything."*, well, that makes sense. If you haven't had the opportunity to experience anything, then you have to just trust in blind faith. I would never ask or expect anyone to "just have faith". That's just not practical.

I believe. That does not mean I believe every account of life after death--I don't believe everything.

Religions and cultures ask us to just "have faith". I believe that we as humans can't believe through faith alone. This is especially true for something very different--a different way of life.

For the most part, our beliefs are based upon **something**. It could be something tangible like a personal experience or simply based on family stories handed down generation to generation.

There are people who choose not to believe even in the face of proof. They describe unexplainable experiences they have had, yet still refuse to allow even the slightest possibility of a belief in the afterlife, or in paranormal activity itself. Why?

To a small segment of the population there is no explanation. They are determined to remain entirely closed to any other possibilities--we cease to exist. Finito, the end. In a literal sense, it is true. It is the end of us, this body, in this life. It is true that someday this will happen to all of us. I also understand that facing one's own mortality is not a popular thought. It can be scary. So, just a thought of death or reading about it, or even facing the death of our loved ones, forces us to consider our own mortality.

Add to this a lifetime of outside influences upon our beliefs. And, let's face it, the proof we're all looking for will not be fully realized until we have actually passed over.

Then what? We hope to communicate our experience with our loved ones, but they aren't listening. We go about day-to-day trying to do things to get their attention but they ignore us. It's great to become a believer after we've passed, but what good is that if no one will listen?

I have spoken to many spirits over the years who told me they would never have believed when they were alive. They have even asked me" *"How do you do that?"*, or my favorite," *You can see me?"*

With all the plausible concepts offered to us, usually supported by little or no evidence to back them up, it is no mystery why we grow to be skeptical. After a while it's easier to believe nothing--even if it (a spirit) comes up and touches you on the arm or plays with your hair. It is just easier to assume it's the wind or your imagination.

People tell me all the time "*I want proof.*" The first thing I tell them is that they need to look at themselves for their own truth. Often, they are blocking any messages that are being directed toward them.

What they are truly looking for are answers I cannot give them. Their questions can be answered only when they allow themselves to take a chance, to open up their senses and to pay attention. It truly is as simple as that.

We're so afraid of thinking that someone who has passed could really be walking alongside us or watching us sleep. We cringe at the very notion of thinking that this can be the case. Some actually find it revolting. These reactions, I believe, are based upon the only experiences most of us have had with death and dying. Most of us only experience death as a sad, even creepy, occasion. We are forced to go visit what was once the body of a loved one lying in a box. And I don't care how many times people will say this, it is simply not true. "*They did a great job with her.*" It is distressing for us to see a dead person lying in a box. Then there is the wearing of black as a sign of mourning. Traveling to the cemetery, a bleak place to say the least, where we pay our last respects and grieve for our loss. Once again, all these steps force us to face our own mortality.

It is also true that TV shows and movie depictions of horribly disfigured creatures walking the earth certainly do not allow us to see death as anything more than gruesome. It is something we definitely want no part of. Who wouldn't be afraid of this?

I have had people tell me of the wonderful relationships they had with a parent, or how beautiful their mother was when she was young. And most also describe their parent(s) as loving and kind human beings. In the next sentence they'll state "*But, I don't want them with me.*", or even "*Can you make them go away?*"

This fear, this disgust, is hard to understand. Here is someone with whom we shared so much life. Someone who nurtured us, loved us and was so important to us is no longer welcome. Why? Because in the minds of the living, they no longer exist. That person is dead.

This is where I come in.

This loving person is still the person you knew, only better. Think about it. They are not going to turn into an angry, roaming spirit here to cause you harm. It just doesn't make sense. They need you and you need them. Let me tell you why. They're good for our health. It's as simple as that.

I continue to study claims that an increase in health can be measured when an individual has more knowledge of the afterlife.

Some would attribute any benefits to an improvement in overall mental outlook alone. Indeed, many of my clients report a decrease in stress and an increase in their overall sense of well-being.

Even discounting the potential for any physical benefit, I am all for improvements in one's outlook.

If replacing ones fears and anxieties with answers, hope and understanding is misguided and wrong, then as the song goes, "*I don't wanna be right.*"

Connecting with the lives of our loved ones is healthy. It is good for us. They help feed our lives and our souls. They give us strength when we are tired. They give us direction when we are lost. They give us more than we give them. The prospect of "death" does not need to be the end of our connections. It doesn't need to be that way. You can make the change now.

You may think that believing is easy for those open to it. It is not. Wanting to believe and truly believing are two different things. Everyone is different and it takes time.

People believe for just as many reasons as they disbelieve.

For some, the hope for the continuation of life is religiously based. The hope of everlasting life in an uninhibited, whole body, free from disease and stress, is a promise made to us. But do people really believe this or do they simply want to believe?

For some, every detail of their lives here on earth is based on this preparation. As discussed previously, many cultures also promise this and caution the believer to live a life of good, to ensure a place and acceptance in the next realm. Every decision made here affects the quality of our experience in the next life.

This can be a daunting task. Who can do everything perfectly? And the guilt of not being able to live up to this standard is astounding. This type of belief system is very restrictive and hard to achieve.

Others believe because they need that assurance they will be with their loved ones again someday when they too pass from this world. They cling to this belief, but in doing so miss out on the opportunity to have relationships with those loved ones now. So they believe in an afterlife per se, but believe that they themselves have to wait until they have passed from this life to experience the bond again. They do not believe they have an ability to connect and renew that relationship now.

Then, there are those that I consider very fortunate. Like myself, there are those who believe because they have seen.

The experience is indescribable and once you have experienced the connection, you will always believe. It is not something you can turn your back on or choose to ignore. There is no changing of the mind once you have experienced your own "proof" from the other side.

You can choose to believe in them or not. You will not dissuade them. They will continue to try to get your attention. It will be your choice whether you choose to hear them. I believe that everyone who has had this opportunity has an obligation to pass it on--to try to help others experience the same connection.

Sometimes you are successful, sometimes you are not. Just keep trying. It's that important.

And with each person you help who tells you," *I sleep better now.*", "*I'm going out with my friends again.*", "*Yes, I talk with her every day.*", etc. you will begin to understand what a wonderful gift this is. And you will know why you need to do this.

I know why I need to do this. Do you?

I have a quote in the beginning of this book that I wrote. It is something I ask everyone to consider. I ask you to consider this now.

"Is it easier to believe what the mind tells you is true, or is it easier to see the truth and then convince your mind otherwise?"

Sydney Sherman.

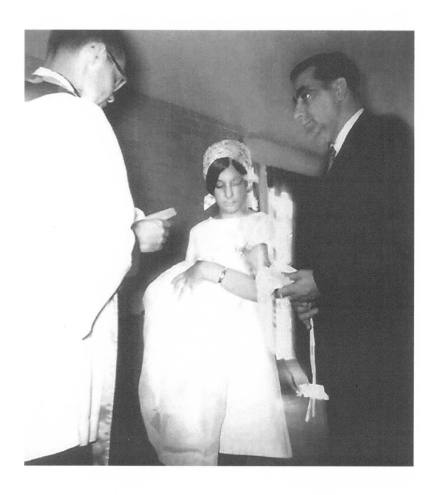

Nick Christening

Chapter 8 How Do They Touch Our Lives ? (Case Histories)... Are They What's Missing?

A number of my clients have graciously agreed to share their stories below. I hope their experiences will give you a view into the process and possibilities of individual readings.

NICK

Nick is a middle-aged executive with two young daughters. He is what some would consider "a man's man".

Nick is not the type to put up with any nonsense. He is someone who refuses to believe in **anything** unless it's black or white. Nick is a challenge.

Nick was raised in an Italian Catholic family. Church and religion were an integral part of the family dynamics. Nick believed in the afterlife and was intrigued in the subject, but had never seen or experienced anything concrete. He believes in Guardian Angels and is accepting of the fact that these Guardian Angels could be loved ones there to watch over him.

He admits to having some strange experiences; of feeling like he's not alone in his room at night. It is his view that this is possibly a female. He cannot see anyone, but experiences a strong sense of feeling that someone is in the room with him.

Nick has described feelings of being completely paralyzed-- not being able to lift his limbs and humming in his ears which lasts for a few minutes. He attempts to speak but cannot. There's a feeling of being pushed down onto the bed as if someone was sitting on him. He states these incidents started to occur in his mid 20's. He denies any trauma at this time that might indicate a psychological cause.

The feelings he described could certainly be caused by a phenomenon called "sleep paralysis". This occurs when the body is trying to come out of REM sleep. The brain is awake before the body reacts.

Or perhaps this is the energy of someone trying to get his attention. Nick had been curious and wanted to find out for himself.

He borrowed my digital voice recorder and placed it in his basement prior to going to bed for the evening. The last thing he stated to me before using the recorder was that he *"just wanted to know they're all right"*. Upon a review of the tape, it appears Nick got his answer in the form of a female voice stating *"I am fine"*. I am happy to say that recently Nick asked me to give him a reading. I hope this means he has come to trust me. I'm glad I (or we) finally got his attention.

Jill Fishing with her Grandpa

JILL

Jill is a young, hard-working mother of a young boy. He is her life. When I sat with Jill she was looking for reassurance that her grandpa was still watching over her. Was he proud of how she was handling her life with her young boy? Was he proud of her decision to be more independent?

I shared with her that her grandpa was with her, that he has always been with her. She had often wondered if he had missed the opportunity to see her son and have a relationship with him.

It was soon apparent that, in fact, he had not missed a moment. He would remark on the similarities between herself as a young girl and her boy. Their personality, their stubbornness and energy. He hadn't missed any of it. In fact, he referred to her son as "Bub". She was glad to know that her grandpa was still with her and that he could see her son. She needed to know that he was watching over him just as he had watched over her so many years before.

Being a young mom of a small boy is not an easy task; she knew her grandpa would be the one person who would make sure everything was okay.

The stories he told about teaching her to fish or tying her first knot were comforting to Jill. She wanted this same nurturing foundation for her son. She needed to know that when she could not be with him, there was somebody that would be keeping a watchful eye over him. Her grandfather was the one person she had wanted, more than anything, to remain a part of her life. It was only natural for her to want to share the companionship of her son with her grandpa. And now she knows he has always been a part of both.

Clayton's Family

Clayton's Grandfather and family

Clayton's Grandma

CLAYTON

Clayton is a young professional who works long hours and tries to make the most of life.

When I met him, he had mixed feelings about life after death and even questions whether there is life for us after we pass. This confusion was based in part on religious views and social opinions that conflicted with his personal beliefs. He needed answers and wasn't sure what to believe.

My first experience with Clayton was, I believe, a starting point. His contact provided some validation of his feelings and an opportunity to resolve the contradictions of his perspectives on communication with the other side.

This seemed to come at just the right time. After our first reading, both Clayton's grandparents passed suddenly. Clayton and his mom were hit very hard by this news. They were not fully prepared for what would come next.

As with most families, decisions had to be made, plans needed to be changed. At a time when they should be coming together, family dynamics got in the way causing discord and disagreements. Clayton and his mom needed to know they were doing the right things.

From the outset, Clayton's grandma and grandpa visited frequently. They offered reassurance on the decisions made and the tasks accomplished. Sometimes they had a lot to say. Sometimes what they said was not what Clayton wanted to hear. Then again, that's how they were. Grandma still doting on her little boy (Clayton was her favorite), and Grandpa cracking jokes in his odd manner.

We have now had several sessions together and Clayton feels confident and more reassured than ever before. All he was looking for was honesty and common sense answers. I feel he has found what he was looking for and I thank him for sharing a very personal experience with me.

Daniella's Mom

Daniella and Her Brother

DANIELLA

Daniella is a young girl with many challenges. Too many challenges for girl her age.

When I met Daniella, let's just say we didn't "click". But I knew her story from the moment I met her. She was one person I felt truly needed me. Not for the curiosity or for the validation necessarily, but for her soul.

She had suffered two great losses in a short period of time. Her young brother, her friend, her little annoyance, was taken from her quickly. Within a few years her mother, struggling from disease, was taken from her as well.

What was left behind was a lot of questions, anger, sorrow, fear and resentment. These losses interfered with every inch of her being. Every girl needs her mother, every sister wants her brother.

I can see the need in her--just as strong was the need of her mom and brother to connect with her. They were feeling **her** loss. They also knew they needed to help her the only way they could.

Danielle's reading was emotional to say the least. It was hard for someone like me not to feel overwhelmed by the grief and loss suffered by this young girl. Every decision she made, everything she did was always accompanied by a question mark. Would her mom approve of her life?, her lifestyle?, her loves?, even her career choice? What would her mom say? What would her mom think?

There comes a time in every young girl's life when the presence of her mom is one of the most important things. This was true for Daniella who had felt all opportunity of this was gone.

During her reading some questions were answered; some wounds healed. This is a chance for a new relationship to be built. Danielle now knows how to communicate with her mom and her brother and to recognize "the little things".

After our reading, Daniella told me how she came home one day from work and found an envelope from the store with pictures of her mother in it. Daniella had never ordered any of these pictures. She actually didn't know these pictures existed, yet the envelope stated the pictures were already paid for. Danielle said "*It was obvious to me it was a sign from my mom.*"

An occurrence like this might have gone unnoticed or disregarded before, but not anymore. The pain is still there. It will take time, but Danielle is strong, stronger than she knows (she gets it from her mother). I will continue to help her. I'm glad to have had the opportunity to get to know her for the wonderful young women she is.

A Christmas Ornament from Ellie's Mom

ELLIE

Ellie is a divorced working mother and grandmother. She enjoys her family, her work and her friends. She is a very warm and caring person. The type of person you can "tell all your troubles to". She can size up anyone faster than anyone I have ever met. One would never know that behind this warm, caring soul is a woman with a family history of conflict and judgment–a legacy of uncaring and unforgiving influences in her life.

When I first met Ellie, we instantly "clicked". She understood me when others didn't. Her abilities as an empath made us partners in another realm that most could not understand.

She did not need me to tell her that spirits exist or that life goes on. She simply needed to have a few questions answered, not only for herself, but for her son and grandchildren as well.

From our first reading, her mom was front and center. Ellie loved her mom, but her mom's love was conditional. It always had been. That was no different after her death. Ellie needed a better understanding of why her mother was the way she was and why her father seemed so disconnected and non-protective.

Ellie knew the underlying condition that plagued her mom, but that didn't make things easier.

Did her mom understand what she was like to live with? Did she care how she made those around her feel?

Ellie always knew she was loved. Times were not always bad. Her mother was not always difficult. I found this to be true during my discussions with her mom as well.

Her mom keeps a watchful eye over her grandson and his children, a loving and protective eye. She also lets her daughter know Mom is with her by doing little things like leaving Christmas ornaments around for her daughter to find.

Ellie has gained a better understanding of the relationship she has with her mother. She knows that her mother's strength is what makes Ellie the person she is today.

She still has questions, but feels the information she has obtained is *"life changing"*. I am very lucky to know Ellie and appreciate the patience and kindness she has shown me. She truly is a special friend.

Ezia's father

EZIA ("Z")

Z, is a fun-loving, creative, vibrant mother of two. She is married and runs her own business. She is the type of person who enjoys living no matter what life wants to throw at her.

When I met Z she had been told about my abilities from a local business. Her initial instinct was one of curiosity more then skepticism, so, she was going to give me a try.

Her hopes were to find out how accurate I was and to see who would come through. She wasn't actually expecting a visit from her father. She and her father had not been close in years. But there he was! And just to be told her dad was still with her was not going to be enough. She needed more proof. Her father chose the way. The only way to give his daughter the proof she was looking for–his personality.

Z's father's personality and exuberance were unmistakable.

It was very easy to see the love of a father in his eyes. His eyes are strong and loving; his wit, quick. The love between this father and daughter was undeniable. He had a lot to say. It was just as important for him to **say** it as it was for his daughter to hear it.

Z is a very special and gifted woman herself. She told me she always wished to have the ability to connect with the lives of those who past.

The desire was such that she even studied to learn how she could open herself up this ability. She has a natural creative personality. Top that with a brilliant aura as well as an open mind. As she continues to practice working with her natural abilities, I have no doubt that, at some point, she will tap into another realm.

I know she will continue to communicate with her father. It is my hope she will continue to encourage her siblings and children to do so as well.

Z's fun loving, free spirit is contagious. And it is her father's spirit that makes her who she is. I thank her for allowing me to meet him and for being such a good friend to me.

Chapter 8 How Do They Touch Our Lives ? (Case Histories)...

Are They What's Missing?

Chapter 9   How Can I Talk to My Loved Ones ?

This is a question I get asked all the time. I tell people, "Just do it!" "Just start talking." Speak to them as you would if they were sitting right next to you--because they are. They understand that this experience is different, but they want communication as much as you do. Usually they are not the problem; we are.

For those who are interested in making a connection and beginning a conversation with a loved one, the first step is to be prepared. There is no better advice I can give. Prepare yourself for an interaction.

Why? Well for one thing you have to question your motives and examine your personal feelings regarding the subject of death.

And you need to decide what it is you want to get out of this experience.

Ask yourself, why do I want to do this? Is it because you think it's cool? Because you want answers? Or, just because, once again, you want to experience the closeness, the bond you shared before with a special someone.

None of the above reasons are wrong. They are all appropriate reasons to initiate this conversation. However, you also need to be ready; ready for the interaction you seek. If you are apprehensive or scared, wait. If you are not sure, wait. Let me explain why. Everyone's feelings are just as different as the reasons for wanting an interaction differ from one another.

And by the way, you can't fail this. There is no right way or wrong way. There's just your way. Define your own niche; your comfort zone. No one can find this for you, but some guidance may bring about some interaction more directly.

This chapter is to give you some simple rules you can follow for guidance. Practice it; play with it and be ready for a wonderful experience. If it doesn't happen the first time, please don't become disenchanted. As I said before, it is usually not them, it's us. You have to find what works best for you. It may take a few attempts, but it is well worth it.

Okay first, find a quiet, relaxed comfortable place where you will not get interrupted. Then start thinking of the person you would like to come through for you.

In the beginning I would start with one person. At first you may be met with several energies. Focusing on a single person may help differentiate between different types of energy you may experience. I want you to relax. Try to remember. How did they smell? What did they look like? How did they feel? Close your eyes if you need to and then ask that loved one if they are there.

As I said before, be patient. It may not happen the first time. Keep your questions small. Allow time for response. Listen carefully. If a word suddenly pops into your head, go with it. What's the worst that can happen?

Let me give an example. A phrase comes into my head—a red car. I'll say "Oh," "Who is asking me about a red car?" Then I wait for a response. Sometimes I get something, sometimes I don't.

This is how it happens. Listen to words that you would normally ignore or push aside. We've all had this happen. Suddenly you find yourself thinking about a word or subject or a familiar name pops into your head for no reason. Most ignore it. I don't.

Okay let's go on to the sense of touch. Another thing I tell people to do is to place your hand or arm out in a relaxed fashion. Ask to be touched, but be precise on what you are looking for. For example, a pat or a rub or maybe a squeeze. Also let them know where you would like them to touch you. Possibly on your fingers, your hand, your wrist or maybe your forearm. Be sure your extremity is relaxed. If you tense up, you may confuse a strained or unrelaxed muscle with the experience. Repeat your requests several times, and give them time to respond.

It's important to examine your expectations. What do you think it would feel like to be touched by a spirit? I find that most people are unsure of what to think. Without any better sources of information, we often base those expectations and feelings on what we have seen on TV and in movies, rather than on facts or genuine accounts. Spirits are usually portrayed as cold. This could not be further from the truth.

It is not even sensible. Think rationally. If spirits are energy and energy is heat; why would they be cold? So let me ask you again: Do you imagine the touch of a spirit would be cold? Or would be warm? When you feel their touch, it will be warm. Some people have described it as a tingling, radiating feeling, with a light amount of pressure. Others describe it as a feeling of closeness to their skin. These are all accurate, normal descriptions. It is what you should expect to feel.

I also caution if you do not feel it, don't say you do. This is a personal experience. It has to be right for you. It has to be genuine. If you pretend to feel it, even because you deeply want to have this experience, you will be missing out on the totality of this wonderful experience. Practice and be patient. It will happen.

If you still have trouble feeling them after some practice, pick a place. Some areas of our physical bodies are more receptive to touch than others and everyone is different. Some people find the wrist is a more sensitive and receptive area. Others feel the forehead or the cheeks work better. That is why I stress this is a personal experience. You need to find what works for you. Remember, there is no need to rush; it's an experience worth waiting for. If you do not feel anything, it's okay. I want this experience to become completely natural for you.

I also caution those who have the desire to take this step to be prepared to be touched.

I know that sounds strange. But sometimes what we ask for is not necessarily what we think it will be. As exciting as this experience is, it may be scary if you're not truly expecting it.

As you focus on your loved one, try to think of the person you are calling just as they were when they were here. Picture them lucid and whole rather than sick, old or scary. Don't think of them in any way other than healthy and happy. Once you've had the opportunity to experience their presence, you'll never forget it.

I think the strongest and most receptive place for a person to feel their loved ones--to experience their touch or embrace, may be the upper body. I have experienced this myself when educating others. A hug, a kiss on the cheek, a stroke of the face, these are excellent areas to try. Spirits are very accommodating. They want interaction as much as you do.

Sometimes closing your eyes can not only help you relax, but can also make it easier for you to enjoy their presence as they come closer to you. If you have ever been laying in a dark room and felt your personal space entered, you may recognize the sensation. If you sense a closeness almost as if someone was standing right next to you (even though there's nobody there), that's probably them.

The power of smell is one of our strongest and sometimes, most reliable, senses. Some spirits are known for a particular scent they can create that identifies them to others. These are usually strong scents. And I would like to tell you that they are all enjoyable, however that would not be true. They can smell like a cigar, a pipe, alcohol or even cigarettes. However, they can also present with lighter hints of different scents such as perfumes, flowers or lotions.

This is another experience that we've all had -- a fleeting moment of a smell that immediately brings us to someone or someplace. Most of us choose to ignore a transitory aroma and dismiss any notion of why it would occur. Hopefully, after reading this book, you will be more apt to try to find a basis for the odor rather than ignoring it.

If a scent brings a certain person to mind, call out their name. If it reminds you of a place, call out the name of the place. You may feel silly, but what is it going to hurt?

I always like to share this story. A little while back, I had a client whose loved one presented with a very strong aroma of Ben Gay. As I mentioned this to the client, she stated that she never knew her grandmother to not smell like Ben Gay. She stated she actually liked the smell. It was comforting and familiar. For her grandma, it was like her cologne.

So far, we have discussed hearing, feeling and smelling. And, as I have never tasted a spirit, that leaves us with seeing.

I leave seeing for last knowing full well that this is probably the most important experience anyone would ever want to have. However, I also understand that very few will ever experience this.

I started ghost hunting many years back, not for my need to find spirits (they have always found me), but for verification. By capturing evidence of their existence, I hoped to enable others to share the same opportunities that I've always had-- to connect with those who have passed.

I have all the state-of-the-art equipment at hand. You name it, and it's in my "arsenal". Each piece of equipment has its own benefit. Even with all the tools, the hardest thing to capture is an apparition. The actual shadow, figure or energy of your loved one is probably the hardest, the most elusive, evidence to obtain.

Unfortunately with today's technology, it is too easy to re-create a photo or video to give it the appearance of spirit type activity. Most photos that I see can be easily explained as other things. However, a doctored photo is not as easy to spot as you would think. And with more sophisticated computer programs, people can become quite creative. All I can ask is that you keep an open mind. An open mind to the fact that the photo you are being shown (or even a photo you've taken yourself) is probably not an actual appearance of the spirit or loved one.

I will touch quickly upon orbs. I personally refuse to look at or even consider orbs as potential paranormal activity. Spirits have never presented to me as an orb. Orbs are reflections of light, bugs, dust or some other manifestation present in our natural environment. Too many people run amok showing off all their pictures of orbs wanting others to believe they've caught a spirit. Please don't allow your need to connect with your loved one to outweigh common sense.

If a spirit is capable of manifesting itself, it will not be out the corner of your eye. It will manifest itself and leave no doubt in your mind of what you just witnessed.

Just as people have preconceived notions of what it would feel like to be touched by spirit, we also have a preconceived notion of what they would look like.

They are not skeletons. They are not disheveled and all females are not dressed in white period clothing. It amazes me how many times I hear people describe the spirits in a particular home as being from a particular period of time. I think they assume old homes, old spirits. It's almost as if people who passed recently are no where to be found. I have gone to many old homes and have experienced no spirit existence. I have also visited newly built homes where the homeowners felt there could not possibly be any presence and found activity. Many forget about the history of the land or the area. Some of my more active homes were newly built, but retained spirits from other structures or property. Once again, a preconceived notion might have blocked us from a meaningful connection.

So we have just briefly discussed what you can expect and what types of things you can do to help in your endeavor.

Having the opportunity to have any type of experience with a loved one is a wonderful thing. You just have to find which works best for you. And just remember, "If you make yourself available, they will come".

Chapter 10 The Reader...
What You Need to Know About Readers

I'm sure you've heard it before. 1 800 psychic, DIAL-A-MEDIUM, or have seen the many signs that litter the streets for mediums, psychics, mystics etc. There is no shortage of those who will tell your fortune for a price. They may even give you a special deal of 2 for 1.

These people are one of the reasons I decided to write this book. As I said in the beginning, there truly are many people who are able to speak to those who have passed. Unfortunately, there are many more who cannot. They prey on people's emotions, watch for clues, present leading questions and even hand out cards to be filled out by the unsuspecting victim prior to the reading. They fail to mention they are requesting information which will be used to fool you into thinking you are getting your money's worth.

I call these people, "Readers". This is derogatory term in the paranormal field used to identify such fraud.

They come in different forms. Some are the small fries, the little people who use basic techniques to get you to give them information and to get your money. Others are the big players who have made a livelihood out of studying personalities, behaviors, gestures and eye movements, all to lure you into a sense of awe. Both are just as dangerous and we will evaluate them here.

First let's discuss the difference between all the different titles that speakers-to-the-dead use. You have your mediums, psychics, psychic mediums, spiritualists, clairvoyants, fortune tellers and more. They all have different techniques which they used to heighten the experience you paid for. Some use crystals, taro cards and Ouija boards. Some will read your palm, use salts, candles and the eye of newt. This is not a complete list of "absolutely essential accessories". By next week there will be other crucial trappings–and "Readers" will readily justify the necessity for all these vital elements.

Now before I anger people, I'm not talking about the actual practices performed by legitimate mediums and the like. Only the frauds. How can one tell?

First, let's discuss just a few of the categories of paranormal interpreters and what they do.

MEDIUMS: To start, a medium has the ability to channel information from those who have passed to the living, usually by means of words, sounds, gestures, etc. Mediums use their energy and the spirit's energy (by a means termed "transference") to aid in the communication. I have been called a medium. I am not sure if that is entirely how I get my information, but if it helps people that I have a title, I am fine with that. Most mediums will use the information that is provided to them by your "peeps", just as I do. They can give you information of what your loved ones are seeing in the here and now **and** in the past. Insight into the future can only be obtained if the person who has passed has this knowledge in the first place.

PSYCHICS: A psychic has the ability to describe events the future may hold--that which has not occurred yet. They can also send us details of events that have already taken place and are able to give account of these events. They can see things that have occurred relative to crimes and disappearances. Psychics have been used by police and crime officials in the solving of many cases. Many psychics also use the energy from the spirits along with their own to gather this information. Some psychics will tell you they do not know the source of their information or just how it comes to them. It might occur by seeing pictures from a book in their head. Some describe it *"like watching a movie play out"*.

A psychic/medium has a combination of the abilities as described above.

SPIRITUALISTS: A spiritualist takes on the role of the spirit, as if seeing through the eyes of the dead, and communicates for them using the spiritualist's body and voice. A strong sense of energy transference occurs here. Spiritualists became popular in the early 1900s. They were used by royalty and others of means to continue a relationship with their loved ones who had passed.

CLAIRVOYANTS: A clairvoyant again channels information through a spirit's energy as a medium does. This term is used interchangeably with medium.

FORTUNE TELLERS: Fortune tellers are usually seen in the carnival setting. They tend to tell you events that will occur in your future usually regarding wealth and love. Their results are not based upon anything scientific. If there is any legitimacy to what they do, I have not seen it. Your expectations should end once they have taken your money, and given you "information" about your future (possibly in a bad foreign accent). What do you do when it does not occur? Try to find them?

EMPATHS: I will also offer up another type of person who may not speak with the dead. However, through their intuition and their feelings, they can read, identify and understand people's feelings. They are called empaths. They don't read the future or predict it; they read people by reading their energy.

Now regardless of title, there are legitimate people with legitimate abilities and those who pretend. And the latter are what I will call "The Readers". They use tricks and they're very good at it. Some of the tricks of their trade will be touched upon now. Also offered are suggestions on how you can avoid being a victim.

Many "Readers" will ask you why you are there. Your answer, whatever it might be, has just given them a key piece of information they can use instead of any results from actual contact. Let me explain. Your response "*I just lost my mother and I want to see if she's with me*". Okay, now if I were a professional "Reader" I would now know that you are looking for your mother and guess what... of course she is here. Why wouldn't she be? You just gave the "Reader" someone to start with. "Readers" don't even have to guess anymore.

Some "Readers" ask you if you have ever had a reading before or what your feelings are about the afterlife. Simple enough question. Harmless enough. However, it is well known that people who have seen psychics or mediums previously have a strong belief in the afterlife. They may be very impressionable and can be made to believe (at least in the moment) that what is being said is true.

I prefer to read for skeptics. A believer sometimes wants **so** much to believe, that they will try to rationalize anything you tell them to make it fit even if it doesn't. Don't fall for that.

Many people have told me that they have been handed a questionnaire (!) to fill out prior (!) to the reading. I find it hard to believe anyone would fall for this, but they do and these "Readers" know that. Their explanation for this is to allow the "Reader" to connect you with your spirit by embracing your personal energy. These questions are bold and blatant. Most people don't realize they're giving the "Reader" everything they need for a "successful" reading. Clients are frequently caught up in the moment. Don't give **any** information. If they are legitimate, they will get what they need from your loved ones and not from you.

Then there is the "Uncomfortable Pause". For those that do not understand what I mean, the "Reader" will usually ask you a question or make a statement and then wait for your response. They will wait and wait. What they are doing is waiting for a nervous statement. This is a ploy that I like to call the "Uncomfortable Pause". You feel you need to say **something**; they want you to say something. They hope you will say something that gives them more information. Just remember that old saying that a very special person once told me. It works every time. *"The next person who speaks... Loses"*. Long periods of silence are awkward and we feel we need to comment, to break this uncomfortable moment. Stay quiet. If they ask you a yes or no question, answer it simply, "yes" or "no". Do not expand on your comment.

That is precisely what the "Reader" is waiting for. They are counting on more information from you and that, later on, you will forget you gave them critical facts.

Now the professional "Readers", the bigwigs, actually spent a lot of time honing their craft. It is actually pretty impressive. They study body language. They study facts about cultures, societies, religions, backgrounds and even common names in cultures. They know the data right down to the percentages of people who die from cancer, heart attacks or other ailments. Oh yes, they do their homework. Let me give you an example--

You come in for reading and you are in your 30s. Statistically, the chances are very good that both parents are still alive as well as grandparents and siblings. Seventy-five percent of people who go to a psychic or medium have siblings. Again, with your age there is a good probability that they are still alive. So I will begin by saying something like. *"You have your great grandparents with you."* Good guess, because logically they have probably passed. Now you are impressed *"How did they know I had great grandparents who have died?"*

They begin their questions and they watch your expressions. No expression equals no direct hit. They change their line of questions. Now your eyebrow rises. They got the recognition response to their statement. They go further now; you clasp your hands; you are clearly uncomfortable; they have hit on another area. You become fidgety, wow, they've got you now. And the whole time you have no idea that **you** are giving them all the answers without opening your mouth. You are caught up in the moment.

They will even use your nationality to gather information from you. If you are Italian, Spanish, German etc., this can all be used to force you to believe that the "Reader" is identifying with you.

Another tactic they employ is to stare the client down. This is very uncomfortable. Just as uncomfortable as the silence. We become flustered. They will also begin to repeat (over and over again) what they want you to believe. This gaze in the field is what they call "the hook" because it can make a client so uncomfortable that they begin talking incessantly while trying to make what the "Reader" has told them fit their situation. Try to look away from the "Reader". You control the situation not them. You're paying them good money, let them work for it.

BIGWIG READERS - This is probably my favorite type of "Reader". I like to call them the "Mathematicians". These heavy-hitters of the "Reader" world are very impressive. These "Readers" will point to a group of people and say that they have someone coming through presenting with problems in their chest. You will always have two or three people in this group who know of someone who has passed from chest issues of some kind. Statistically, in a group of approximately 10 people, eight of those will probably have had someone close either have a lung or a heart problem. What do they do? They raise their hands. The "Reader" scopes them out. Then they go quickly to the next question. Again, statistically of these eight people who have raised their hands probably five have had loved ones who actually passed away from their condition. Then the "Reader" will usually state a gender -- male or female. They will usually pick a male as percentage-wise there are less men than women. Now they are probably left with two. They have their two victims. They can easily point to one of the two and asked them "Who has passed?" The target (victim) will probably tell them because they feel they were picked out of a group, instead of realizing the "Reader" used the law of averages and some good math, to lie. How impressive; how disgusting.

Now you may wonder how I know all this. And you would be right to wonder. If I know all this maybe I use the same techniques. I will tell you. I too have studied them, as they have studied you. I can recognize them very quickly and now, so can you.

A good interpreter, a legitimate reader, will clearly tell you that they do **not** want any information from you. They will remind you when they ask you a question to answer only "yes" or "no" and not to respond further. They will look away from you when speaking with your loved ones as not to intimidate you or appear to be gathering information from you by your gestures. A good reader will tell you that the information that is coming through should **not** be difficult or hard for you to validate. They should educate you on the process and allow you to ask questions. The experience should **not** leave-you shaking your head and asking questions or feeling that the money you've just paid was wasted.

You should always tape-record your session or ask that someone be present to take notes. You need to be free to enjoy your reading. No one who is legitimate would take issue with that. Those who would take issue with recording your reading do not want you to be able to look back at how they handled you and your reading. Your reading experience should be relaxed and welcoming.

A good interpreter will help you to understand and teach you how to have the experience with your loved ones. They can identify the capabilities of your loved ones: i.e. touching, speaking, hearing etc. You should feel that the information you were provided with was obtained by communication between your loved one and the medium **not** from you. This information should not be general in nature, but descriptive and personal. It should not be information that a medium would ever know or guess.

Your reading should take place in a quiet room. As I said, a relaxed environment is a must. Dim lighting, curtains in different colors, lights with multicolor shades or wall rugs are not necessary. Once again, these "staged settings" are meant to put you in an easily suggestible frame of mind. It's meant to heighten your experience--to put you "in the moment". All of this has nothing to do with you and your reading, and is not necessary. Money should never change hands until your experience has concluded. You would never buy a garment or any other item without checking it out first. If they ask you for payment before your reading, simply state "No".

A truly legitimate reading is between the reader, the client and your loved ones. Stay clear of those who look more like they are off the pages of a book...they *probably* are not real.

Now as I said before, they (the charlatans) are out there and they're not going to go away. But you do not have to fall victim to their games. If it doesn't feel legit; it's not. To experience a reading is a very natural thing. That's how you should feel. And once you have felt it, you will never forget the experience. I truly believe that it changes lives.

Chapter 11 More About the Reader...
The Energy of Things

As if taking your money was not enough, some myths or misconceptions are made up to fool people into giving up their possessions as well as their fee.

The idea of a person's essence or spirit being attached to an item is **not** a myth. Residual energy from the previous owner of an item or home can and does remain. It's like an imprint of that person's energy which is left behind.

The residual energy of a possession **cannot interact** with us nor can contact be made with the spirit attached to a thing. The spirits do not see you. What you experience is simply a repeating of an action taken by them similar to replaying of a tape recorder over and over again. So to be clear, the imprinting of one's energy into an area or an item **is** truly possible.

A hairbrush owned by your grandmother, a favorite serving dish of your mother's can retain their personal energy and, in fact, if their true energy resides in the area where this item is located, they do visit it and cling to it.

However, this is quite different from those who would have you believe that these items not only invite access of **your** loved ones to your home and your family, but also allow contact by **other** beings, (usually not so pleasant or nice to you) into your surroundings. These people will gladly "*help*" you right out of your belongings. They remove these items "*to rid you of the evil*". They can be quite convincing. And who would want to bring "*evil*" into their home and risk injury to their family? No one. And these deceivers know this. So, they take on the "*burden*" of these items.

Now, don't you feel better? Of course you do. Oh, did I mention that most of the items that appear to cause harm and ill will are usually valuable? So by "*helping*" you, they are "*helping themselves*".

My purpose of this book was for revelation. My hope is for a better understanding of what is true and what is nonsense. In the end **you** decide.

Claims of allowing evil spirits or harmful energies into your home are disingenuous to say the least. That is not to say that this does not occur, but simple EVP (electronic voice phenomena) sessions, photo taking, speaking to our loved ones or asking for signs does not bring about a malevolent intent and open us up to "*all the evil of the world*".

Make your requests genuine and directed toward a person or persons known to you, or, to the ones you hope to contact.

Use of negative energy items, such as a Ouija board **is** allowing a "gate", so to speak, to be opened by its mere use. The triangular piece of this game has been noted in some writings as a reference to the "*triad of the devil and his followers*" in a traditional reference to Hades. The signs on the board have been used in demonic practices.

The use of energy transference through the fingertips of the users can be highly provocative in nature. The fingertips are the highest point of energy transference for the living. It is thought to increase the blood flow of all the participants. The contact with each other's increased energy can be magnified, thus causing a "super energy".

This is different from sitting in your home and asking simple direct questions. You are not inviting anyone **outside** in. Any of **your** attempts to contact **your** "peeps" **does not** open a gateway for evil. This does not happen. That is why I do not like the word "haunted". It creates a negative image of these communications. A home is visited. A person or item is visited. See, pleasant and accurate.

So please, hold onto your items. It is highly unlikely your possessions are the cause of anything that may or may not be occurring in your home and even less likely they hold any evil intent. Grandma's silver, and Mom's golden pendant need to stay with you and not end up in the hands of someone wanting to rip you off.

Chapter 12 Touched by an Angel...
How Do They Help Us ?

I could probably write an entire book just on all the stories people have told me over the years where they've encountered situations that have altered their lives.

The essence of their claims was the same. They felt it was their guardian angel or their loved one who had helped out in the course of some very serious situations or who brought them through devastating times.

How does this happen? Which spirits will reside with you? How is all this determined? The answers to these questions are not known. I will say that most of the time, the spirit or spirits we have with us are beneficial.

But how beneficial they are to us, in itself, is a whole other story.

There have been many times I've given readings to people where the loved one who accompanied them did not look like the best match—at least on the surface. At times I have been left scratching my head trying to figure out what benefit my client received from the accompanying energy. Perhaps it is not necessary for us to know. It is not a stretch to say that sometimes we don't know what is good for us or what we truly need. And even though their intent, at the time, may not be apparent, it is usually what they do behind the scenes that matters.

This chapter is a compilation of some of the accounts of those people I've encountered along the way. They come from people of all walks of life. Some subjects have always been believers; some became believers after their encounters.

I decided to share four stories with you. I picked each one to give my readers a demonstration of the different types of ways spirits interact with us and keep us safe. These accounts are a true and accurate testament to the love and the bond that ties us together.

PROTECTOR: This first story relates to one of several ways we might be protected.

In the fall of 2003, a young couple and their six-month-old baby left their home to go visit a friend two hours away. The friend's aunt was recovering from surgery and they thought the presence of the baby would bring her some cheer. After their visit they got back onto the road at about 5 PM for the 2 hour drive home. They were tired from the trip and just wanted to relax.

They pulled into the driveway and proceeded to unpack all the gear. Walking slowly up the side walk and up the three front steps, the husband held the baby and put the key in the door.

The lock, which ordinarily opened easily, would not budge. After several attempts he handed the baby to his wife. He held the door knob with one hand while he tried the key again with his other hand. Still, the door would not open. He checked to see if it was the right key; it was. As he attempted again to get the door open the key was "slapped" from his hand with such force that it landed in the hedges several yards away.

He and his wife were startled. At that moment, the wife saw a shadow move by the front window. She whispered to her husband *"There's someone in the house!"* They immediately went back to the car without turning on the lights. They backed down the driveway quietly and pulled down the street. Only when they were a safe distance away, did the husband use his wife's cell phone to call 911. When the police arrived, they rushed into the house and found a man attempting to pour gasoline around the first floor. When the police encountered him in the home, he also had a long deer knife and gun.

What would have happened if they had entered the home and caught him in the act? What about the baby? But, they had been unable to get into the house. Inexplicably, the key they had used so many times before didn't work. How would you explain the key being slapped with such force that it flew through the air a distance of several yards into the hedges. Luck? Maybe...

After the incident, the couple went to retrieve the key from the hedges. The key was not in the hedges; not on the lawn or anywhere nearby. When they returned to the porch, they found the key neatly placed just on top of the hand rail right where they could find it easily. And, as you may have guessed, when the husband attempted to open the door with that same key, it now opened immediately--just as it had done so many times before.

This report of activity is similar to many others where an object is not only moved, but moved quite a distance and with force. Spirits use an "energy transference" to affect physical items. They are able to use their energy to cause an item to "fly" into the air. Hence, the behavior of the key. Spirits are actually very rational in their attempt to block whatever movement or action they wish to stop. When unable to get our attention in other ways, sometimes "peeps" take the measures in their own hands.

A GUARDIAN: The following story offers another confirmation of the protective nature of those who share a bond with us.

These events took place in October 2007. A woman was late for an after-work Halloween party with her co-workers. Nothing was going right. Her costume choice was a leotard-clad cat, but, at the last moment in her hurried attempts to make up time, her leotard ripped. Frustrated with the evening's occurrences, she hastily got into her car to drive the 15 minutes to the nearest store in an attempt to find another suitable leotard.

Normally a cautious driver, she took chances veering into and out of traffic, running yellow lights, trying to make up time. During this time her cell phone started ringing from its spot on the car seat next to her. But each time she picked it up, she heard only static before the phone went dead. Figuring this was her friends trying to find out why she was late and where she was, she became even more aggravated by the noise of the phone calls. When she finally reached her destination, a Rite Aid, she got out of the car. As she closed the door, her cell phone began ringing again. She reached into the car and grabbed the phone off the seat. She looked at the phone before she answered it, but there was no number listed. As she answered the phone she heard a familiar voice saying" "*Stay in the car, Julia.*" followed by increased static.

As she continued to say "*Hello, hello*" she couldn't help but say "*Mom?*" Even though her mom had passed away more than five years before, the voice was **so** familiar.

All of a sudden she heard what sounded like a firecracker go off followed by another and then another and then another. She jumped back into her car and locked the doors. The phone was still in her hand, but all she could hear was static in the background. Soon there were police sirens and flashing lights surrounding the Rite Aid. The noise was so loud it was deafening. Several police officers ran into the Rite Aid. When one came alongside her car and knocked on the window, he asked if she was okay. "*Yes*" she said. Still confused by what had occurred, and too shaken-up to go to the party, she went home.

The next day she learned from a newscast that a man, distraught over losing his job, had killed three people in the store and then killed himself. If she had been in the store, what would have happened?

She then remembered the phone call and the voice that sounded so much like her mother telling her to stay in the car. She didn't want to believe her mom could be talking through the phone. Could her mom be protecting her still? Julia asked the phone carrier to check her phone service and her phone for any mechanical issues. Everything checked out fine, however, the call log that she requested showed 4 calls, every one in succession for a number that was nonexistent. This has never happened again.

You may have heard that spirits can use their energy and the white noise from electrical appliances, (usually radios or TVs) to communicate with us. I have no doubt with the continued use of cell phones we will hear more similar stories--a familiar voice on the cell phone--calls coming from apparently, nowhere. Was this Julia's mother? I believe it was. It reminds me of the line from the movie <u>Ghosts</u> *"The love you have here doesn't die, you take it with you."* And as we all know, a mother's love is "unconditional, and forever".

THROUGH OUR DREAMS: I felt it was important to add this next story to widen the landscape. Most people have yet to experience communication with "peeps", but I believe we've all had dreams in which our departed loved ones appear. Many dreams contain messages--words or images--telling us things that later come true to some degree. Perhaps a spirit version of a premonition. Spirits will use whatever device or means necessary to get your attention. If you won't pay attention when you're awake, possibly you'll pay attention while you sleep. I believe this is what happened in the next story.

In December 2004, the young woman was experiencing her first pregnancy. She was in her seventh month and she was alone. Her Coast Guard husband had been sent for training and would be gone for two weeks. She wasn't concerned. She was glad the pregnancy had proceeded without incident. She was healthy and got plenty of rest.

Nonetheless, she always worried about complications. Like the complications that took her mother from her when she was only four days old. She had never been told what type of complications; it was too hard for her father to speak of.

She had never actually seen what her mother looked like. Her father was so distraught over her death, he removed all pictures of her mom from the home. He remarried when the young woman was only 14 months old.

She was busy getting ready for the holidays when she started getting what she described as a twinge in her belly. It seemed to go away after a few minutes and wasn't painful, so she didn't consider it cause for alarm. It was something she would bring up to her doctor when she saw him for her appointment in two days. She was excited to be getting her third ultrasound. She enjoyed seeing her pregnancy progress. When she went to the doctor, she told him of her experience. After asking a few questions, the doctors stated it was probably just the pressure of ligaments from her uterus and nothing to worry about.

He gave her a clean bill of health. She went home pleased and continued with all the holiday preparations.

That afternoon the twinges became more frequent and more intense. She called her mother-in-law and told her what she was experiencing. After reassurance from her mother-in-law, she decided to just lie down to get some rest. She soon fell asleep. In her dream a woman presented herself to her. She could barely see her. She looked distorted and fuzzy, but she heard the woman very clearly telling her to *"Get the baby out!"* The dream woman repeated this message over and over and over again. When the mom-to-be awoke she reflected *"What a strange dream"*, but then thought no more about it.

The next day the twinges were replaced with sharp stabbing pains that increased in intensity. When they didn't stop as the day wore on, she again called her mother-in-law who instructed her to call the doctor. The doctor asked her to come in for an evaluation. After her appointment, which included another ultrasound, her doctor stated everything was normal. She had nothing to worry about. The baby was larger than they had expected, so she should expect more pulling on the ligaments which would mean a little discomfort. The doctor was reassuring. He restated his belief in his previous diagnosis.

She returned home. Now, a little concerned, but relieved in the fact that two ultrasounds came back normal. Late that night as she slept, she again dreamt of this woman. She could see her better this time. She couldn't help but notice what a pretty smile she had. The birthmark on her left hand also remained in her memory. Again the woman was telling her to "*Get the baby out*" repeatedly--over and over.

When she awoke, she felt a sense of panic and urgency. She had the impression something wasn't right. She decided to go to the hospital directly. (She told me later she thought it was a mother's intuition.) At the hospital, an emergency cesarean section was done and the baby was born. They whisked the baby away from the new mother. Apparently there **had** been a problem. The young mother's placenta had ruptured. If she hadn't gone to the hospital when she did, she would not only have lost the baby, but she would have bled to death.

A few weeks later while visiting, she told her aunt about the dreams and asked about the details of her own mother's death. The aunt stood up with a tear in her eye and went and retrieved a picture, a very young picture, of her mother. There stood the woman from her dream with the pretty smile **and** the small birthmark on her left hand. She was amazed to be finally meeting not only her mother but the woman from her dream. But the story doesn't end there. She then learned from her aunt that her own mother died from blood loss after she had delivered her. Her mom's placenta had ruptured as well.

As I said before, spirits will use whatever means necessary to get a message to you. I have no doubt that this was a loving mother who had always guided and watched her young child, a young child who never knew her.

Now for a silly one!!

A MOM IS A MOM FOREVER:

This account is proof that old wives tales are true, and the mother's nagging should be heeded.

In 1979, a young man of 17 named Mark was about to find out how a boy always needs his mother.

Mark was only 14 when he lost his mother to cancer. He would tell everyone how, when she was alive, his mother used to pick out his clothes (right down to his underwear) every day for him before school. He would say she was very "doty". But you could always tell even with all his joking that he missed his mother very much.

He said she was from the old school and she would always tell him to make sure he wore clean underwear because you never know what can happen. "You don't want to be embarrassed." she would say. Apparently, she felt he **still** needed to be told.

One day, Mark was late for school so he quickly threw on his clothes without showering and ran downstairs to get his car keys. On the last step of the landing was a fresh, clean pair of tidy whities. He didn't pay much attention as he was late. He grabbed the keys and ran to the kitchen to get some juice. On the kitchen table was another clean, freshly folded pair of tidy whities. A little puzzled he shook his head, drank his juice and went to the living room to get his books and backpack. Sitting there on the couch was another pair of tidy whities. Mark caved in. I remember him telling me he looked up to the heavens and said "*Okay, Mom, I get it.*" Even though he was late, he felt his mom was trying to get a message to him. He ran upstairs to replace his previously worn underwear with one of the freshly folded pair provided. Now he could go to school.

Running late he parked his car in a makeshift parking spot next to a trash can with his window open. He figured he would move it after class since it would only be about 45 minutes. After that class he went back to his car to move it to a more appropriate place. He hopped in the car, closed the door and started to drive off. He began feeling something crawling up his legs. Then he starting to feel stinging–multiple stings one after another to both his legs. It was very painful. He was attempting to move his car while trying to roll up his pants legs to see what was stinging him, but the pain was increasing. He threw the car into park and jumped out. He was unable to see what was stinging his legs. The pain was so severe that he pulled his pants off and threw them on the ground. With the pants, were dozens of bees. He was relieved that the bees had finally stopped stinging him. That is, until he realized that he was surrounded by schoolmates (all outside as they changed classes), watching his dance in only his tidy whities! And in between the jeers of laughter by his schoolmates, he looked up to heaven and said *"Okay, Mom, I got it. Love you Mom."*

Now this account, while humorous in nature, is significant for the importance it holds for a son who missed his mom. Her leaving his tidy whities out in different locations was not necessarily her way of ensuring he changed his clothing, but was more of a validation. This was Mom's way for him to know that she was still there for him.

This type of object manipulation or the movement of an object from one place to another is very common. An individual's personal article is the best item to be used for many reasons. But I think for Mark, given his personal relationship with his mother and the many jokes they had over his tidy whities over the years, these items were precisely the right means for the message. Mark needed to know that his mom was still there. Now, there was no doubting she was always there and always will be.

These are just a few of the many stories I have gathered over the years that could have been included in the book. I just wanted to give you an opportunity to see 4 different types of ways our loved ones can and do use the environment, their energy or whatever they can to get their messages to us. Now, they are doing their part...We have to do ours.

Reader Checklist... Who Should You Choose to Help in Your Own Journey ?
Watch for the Tricks ~ Avoid the Charlatans

There are many who prey on people's emotions. Watch for the clues: leading questions, requests for information prior to the reading, uncomfortable pauses that encourage you to fill in the blanks. Keep these in mind so you can get a legitimate reading.

A Questionable Reader

Reader tells you events that will occur in your future–especially regarding wealth and love	They may just tell you what they think you want to hear.	Be skeptical
Reader asks you why you are there.	Your answer, gives key information to read **you**, not your loved one.	Don't offer ANY information.

Reader asks you if you have ever had a reading before. Or reader asks your feelings about the afterlife.	The reader uses this to gauge your gullibility.	Don't give any information
Reader offers a questionnaire to fill out prior to the reading.	They should be able to get all they need from your loved ones not from you.	Don't give any information
Reader provides long, "uncomfortable pauses".	Reader hopes you will fill the silence with clues.	Don't fall for it. Let there be silence
Reader asks a yes or no question.	Answer it simply yes or no, do not expand on your comment	Be skeptical

Be wary of readers who watch your body language, focus on cultural or religious identity or speak of problems with a general body area like the chest	They do their homework. They study your behavior and know all the probability statistics on illness, death etc.	Don't let them fool you with general speculations.
Watch out for readers who "stare you down".	Don't respond by talking. Look away if it's easier.	Don't let them trick you into offering more information.

The Good Reader or Medium

Reader tells you **not** to offer information.	Think carefully before you offer facts inadvertently.	👍
Reader reminds you to answer only "yes" or "no"	Answer **only** yes or no.	👍
Will not ask for money upfront.	And don't pay them until the conclusion of the reading	👍
Provides a relaxed environment, quiet room	Try to stay as relaxed and open as possible.	👍
Gives specific, descriptive and personal information, not generalities	Record or have someone take notes so you can remember the details.	👍

Information comes from your loved one through the medium, not from you.	Hopefully, you'll receive information that could ONLY come from that individual.	👍
Identifies the capabilities of your loved ones	Are they capable of communication via speech, touch, etc.?	👍
Helps you to understand and teaches you how make contact with your loved ones on your own	Record or have someone take notes so you can remember these suggestions as well.	👍

The Family Gallery

Cleo Sherman Fitch and Florence Hildebrandt

Marie Celia

Philomena Helen Celia Arline Patricia Bates

Philomena Helen Celia   Edward C. Bates   Arline Patricia Bates

Cleo Sherman Fitch

Pop Pop, my grandfather

Herriet Ames, my Great, Great Grandmother

TESTIMONIALS The Impact of Conversations

A few testimonials–

The impact of our conversations

"I love watching the exchange between our world and the spirit world when Sydney is giving a reading, I am fascinated by it!"

"Her accuracy is right on target, too!"

E.L.

"Medium Sydney Sherman is amazing, a little scary. I was reluctant to have a reading with her, but within the first 10 minutes of her talking to relatives that have passed, I was blown away. The things that she told me instantly convinced me of life after death and... gave me comfort in a way I have never known. I think I have been blessed to have crossed her path and comforted by what I now know about death and people who have passed. It's a wonderful thing to know for certain that loved ones are OK; the things that Sydney told me were things I have never told anyone, not even my closest of friends, it actually took my breath away... Thanks Sydney, I feel that many things I had worried about with my family or myself have gone away, and now I have such a better understanding about life after death".

B.B.

"Thank you, thank you, thank you. The reading you

gave yesterday was so helpful to my GF. The book thing was priceless as even I didn't know about that. You're good."

CSP

"Another great reading by Medium Sydney Sherman. I'm in awe with your talent Sydney!!!! Every time I have a reading, I walk away with a calmness about the other side, and this time I brought my best friend to share in your gift!! What a great experience, you are truly blessed and so are we to have the opportunity to have a reading with you!!! I thank you from the bottom of my heart !!! "

Billy

"Thank you Sydney Sherman Medium.

The reading that my sisters and I received was amazing... You were able to connect with our loved ones so easily. The information was so detailed and accurate we all felt as if our family members were right there talking and communicating as if they had never left. This was especially surprising for my sister, a firm skeptic....she can't stop talking about it... I hope that you truly understand how much you do for people... you are a gift!!!"

BCC

"I had the opportunity to have a reading with Syndey

Sherman about a year ago. All I can say is "WOW"! I come from a long line of disbelievers, if I can't touch it, it doesn't exist.

Part of the reason I went to Syndey was one of curiosity and hope. Hope that I could find out what truly happened to my mother. A family secret kept secret to long. I was stunned when Syndey told me she needed no info from me. She did this "cold".

I was caught off guard by what she knew. Shocked and moved. She was kind and gentle in her comments through what was a very emotional time.

The info she gave me was enough to get the secret out. She was 100% accurate.

I will never forget what she gave me that day. I am now a believer."

CGM

"Fantastic and Amazing!!! I never miss a day now communicating with my loved ones. Everything Sydney taught me to do has helped me feel their love and energy. I have always felt alone, now I feel surrounded by love and enjoy everyday!"

S.E.

"When I found out that Sydney was writing a book, I had to write a little note to let others know how life-

changing my experience was. I was not a believer. As far as I was concerned, life ended here. Until I had my own experience with Sydney. No one knew about a hidden secret that I kept locked away for over 30 years. Sydney did. I was so impressed I began practicing what I was taught. I now experience life differently, and tell others of my transformation. I am very grateful to Sydney for her help!!" J.C

Notes Page

Notes Page

Notes Page

Notes Page

Notes Page

Notes Page

Notes Page

Notes Page